I am speaking now to you Gentiles: . . .
Some of the branches of the cultivated
olive tree have been broken off, and
a branch of a wild olive tree has been
joined to it. You Gentiles are like
that wild olive tree, and now you share
the strong spiritual life of the Jews.
So then, you must not despise those who
were broken off like branches. How
can you be proud? You are just a branch;
you don't support the roots—the roots
support you. . . . You Gentiles are like
the branch of a wild olive tree that is
broken off and then, contrary to nature,
is joined to a cultivated olive tree.
The Jews are like this cultivated tree; and
it will be much easier for God to
join these broken-off branches to
their own tree again.
Romans 11:13, 17-18, 24
Today's English Version

The Olive Tree Connection

John Fischer

InterVarsity Press
Downers Grove
Illinois 60515

InterVarsity Press is the book-publishing division of Inter-Varsity Christian Fellowship,
a student movement active on campus at hundreds of universities, colleges
and schools of nursing. For information about local and regional activities, write
IVCF, 233 Langdon St., Madison, WI 53703.

Distributed in Canada through InterVarsity Press, 860 Denison St., Unit 3, Markham,
Ontario L3R 4H1, Canada.

Cover illustration: Roberta Polfus

ISBN 0-87784-848-3

Printed in the United States of America

Library of Congress Cataloging in Publication Data
Fischer, John, 1946-
   The olive tree connection.

   Rev. ed. of: Sharing Israel's Messiah.   c1978.
   Bibliography: p.
   1. Missions to Jews.   2. Judaism—Relations—
Christianity.   3. Christianity and other religions—
Judaism.   4. Judaism—Essence, genius, nature.
5. Jews—History—20th century.   I. Title.
BV2620.F57   1983   266   83-12645
ISBN 0-87784-848-3

17	16	15	14	13	12	11	10	9	8	7	6	5	4	3	2	1
95	94	93	92	91	90	89	88	87	86	85	84	83				

Acknowledgments

There are many people to whom I owe much
gratitude for their part in this volume:

George and Marianne Fischer, my parents, who
    brought me up in a way that made it all possible;

Patrice, my wife, who stood by me and encouraged
    me and provided insights along the way;

Sandra Keck, who put up with my scrawling to
    type the manuscript;

A number of men who helped shape my thinking:
    Louis Goldberg, Richard Longenecker, Walter
    Kaiser and James Hutchens.

INTRODUCTION: DO
YOU HEAR VOICES?

We live in a noisy society. The noise of planes, trains, buses and cars imposes itself on us. Other sounds deluge us as well: the record player, radio and TV. Newspapers and magazines compete for our attention. But, if we listen carefully, voices rise above all this clamor, calling for our attention.

The voice of a Jewish scientist whispers, "The Jewish nature and soul needs to know God. This is its purpose on earth. Our souls are looking for God and are trying to know God, and no one has told them." A sharp rebuke comes out of the tumult, "This mission business is just like murder. We might as well lose one to Hitler as to the Christians." A bumper sticker in Israel blares its message: "Israel, trust in God." As if in anguish a rabbi's voice rises, declaring that evangelism "produces a stifling, suppressive climate, intrudes on the privacy of Jews, plans their quick liquidation and extinction and shelters anti-Semitism."

Another rabbi speaks out, "This is the time when Messiah will come. He might even come tomorrow." Through the long corridors of time the voice of Zechariah the prophet somberly echoes that prior to Messiah's coming, "two-thirds of all the nation of Israel will be cut off and die."

In the momentary stillness the Messiah's command rings out, "You will be my witnesses, beginning in Jerusalem." In response an evangelical scholar laments, "But the church has for centuries often completely neglected the Jew, and during long periods of time never gotten to Jerusalem at all. This is a tragic and lamentable fact. It is a sin to be confessed and repented of."

Almost in concert two other voices rise. The first, an outstanding biblical teacher from the past, cries, "The attitude of the church to the Jews was almost willfully aimed to strengthen them in their antipathy to the Gospel. The church still owes the Jews the actual proof of its truth. Is it surprising that the Jewish people are such an insensitive and barren field for the Gospel? The church itself has drenched it in blood and then heaped stones upon it." The other, a Jewish voice from the present, booms out, "Psychologically, Christianity is too intimately involved in Jewish minds with the guilt of the Holocaust [the extermination of six million Jewish people during World War II] for Jews to be able to speak or listen freely to it, and the silence of organized Christianity during the Six-Day War has only increased those emotional barriers."

Nevertheless, a voice rings out in challenge, "You Christians, though a wild olive branch, have been grafted into the natural olive tree of the Jewish people. Now you share in the nourishing sap of the olive tree. Don't boast about your position. Rather be grateful. Remember, you don't support the tree; the tree supports you."

Out of the confusion of voices comes the statement of a rabbi, "Two to three thousand Jews are accepting Jesus as Messiah every year."

Come learn the lesson of the voices.

1. Many Jewish people want to know God more personally but will oppose evangelism as a threat to their survival.

2. Numbers of Jews expect Messiah to come and rule the earth, but Zechariah reminds us of a great slaughter of Jewish people to take place prior to that time. God's message must get to them before this.

3. The Messiah himself commanded that Jewish people be given priority in the spread of his message, but his followers have often neglected his instruction.

4. The history of Christian persecution of the Jews has closed their ears to the Christian message. They need to hear the gratitude and love of a people who now share their rich heritage.

5. Jewish people do respond to the Messiah's message when it is sensitively presented in a Jewish way, not threatening their survival or compromising their identity.

Voices all around us constantly clamor for our attention. Out of the confusion comes a still, small voice, the voice of God's love for the Jewish people: "They must be told!"

You who have been connected into the olive tree, are you listening?

1
WHY COMMUNICATE
THE BIBLICAL MESSAGE?

In addition to four wars in thirty years, recent crises have focused much attention on the Middle East. Some people have shown political or economic concern; others' attention stems from simple curiosity. However, followers of Jesus of Nazareth often have a unique reason for their interest; namely, the relationship of Israel and biblical prophecy. Evangelicals repeatedly, often heatedly, discuss this topic. Yet the interest in the Israel of prophecy seldom translates into practical concern for the Israel of today or for the Jewish people as a whole. For example, during the Yom Kippur War in 1973, an Israeli rabbi voiced the disappointment of many Jews in an open letter to "A Christian Brother."

I have to say what is on my mind, because insofar as your rela-

Old Testament biblical references are usually to the Harkavy translation of the Jewish Scriptures (New York: Hebrew Publishing Company, 1951). The verse numbering may differ slightly from other translations. New Testament quotations, unless otherwise noted, are my own translation.

tionship to my people is concerned, I cannot feel that you have carried out the ideals we share. . . . I am horrified at you for saying nothing—again—or issuing statements in which you preserved your simon-pure neutrality. . . . No one has ever been prepared to fight for us. No, that is the wrong way to put it. No one has been prepared to acknowledge our absolute right to all the privileges of life granted to others. . . . We waited for a word of support from you. You talked about "Israeli triumphalism." . . . My thoughts went to Israel's youth, with whom I work every day. I know their abhorrence of war, their horror at having to kill, their deep sorrow at the loss of their dearest comrades, their passion for learning and building. . . . How can you explain your silence following the Syrian, Egyptian, Russian well-planned, brilliantly executed and murderously armed assault on the Day of Atonement?

Attitude Barriers to Communication

Christians give various reasons for this lack of concern for and interest in communicating the biblical message to Jewish people. Some might say, "God is finished with the Jewish people; he set them aside because of disobedience and unbelief." But does the Bible teach this? Isaiah 49:14 makes the complaint that God has set the Jews aside. The next verses contain an enlightening response: "Does a mother neglect her nursing child and not show him love?" Hardly ever. "Yet, even though this might happen," God says, "I won't act this way to you, Israel." He adds that the people of Israel are permanently imprinted on the palms of his hands, where he cannot forget them. Further, the picture of Jerusalem is always in his "mind's eye." Jeremiah 31:34-36 makes an even stronger statement. Here God says that only under certain conditions will he reject the Jewish people for their disobedience. These conditions include the measuring of the universe, the thorough exploration of the earth's foundations, and the abolition of laws of nature such as the cycle of the tides and the course of the sun, moon and stars. Since none of these conditions has ever been realized, God has not set aside the Jewish people.

The New Testament reinforces this. Romans 3:3-4 asks, "Didn't the unbelief of the Jewish people nullify their place in God's purpose?" The passage answers with the strongest possible no in the Greek language (the original language of the New Testament). Romans 11:1-2 asks a slightly different question, "Did God reject his people?" and answers with the same strong no. Later in the same chapter (v. 29) Paul declares that God's choice of the Jewish people cannot be revoked.

"But still," some might respond, "the Bible does say that blindness has come on Israel." This is true according to Romans 11:25. But this passage indicates that this blindness is only partial. In fact, verse 5 points out the existence of a remnant, a number of Jewish people who have not turned their backs on God. The increase in this number today confirms the point of verses 25-26; the blindness is only temporary.

Still another objection might remain: "The Jewish people have rejected Jesus." The leaders, the religious-political establishment, did refuse to accept Jesus as Messiah. Yet a great number of individuals accepted him. Luke 23:27 records that crowds of Jews cried because of his execution. Thousands, and later tens of thousands, trusted him after his resurrection (Acts 2:41; 4:4; 21:20), and this included many of the leaders (Acts 6:7). According to the Jewish historian Neander, one million Jewish people accepted Jesus as Messiah in the first century alone!

Will Jewish people today listen to the biblical message? One Jewish organization leader, Joseph Hoffman Cohn, said, "The astonishing truth is that where Jewish work is efficiently and ably carried on, the actual results are some 3 1/2 to 1 as compared to Gentile results—money, population and effort being equal." Not all Jews will accept Jesus as Messiah, but then not all Gentiles will either.

So it is not a fruitless task to share the biblical message with Jewish people. Actually, there are several important reasons for Christians to have an active concern for Jews and to communicate Messiah's message to them.

A Command to Follow
First, there is a command to keep. Jesus set the pattern by both example and precept in Luke 24:47 and Acts 1:8. (Compare this with the apostles' own understanding of Jesus' statement, Acts

13:46; Rom 1:16.) Simply stated, the message should be shared with the Jewish people first. Many people object to this concept, but the apostles certainly knew what it meant. They so understood Jesus' command that for the first several years of their work, they confined their witness to Israel. Later, everywhere they went, they still shared the message with Jewish people first. Even Paul, who considered himself the apostle to the Gentiles (Rom 11:13), shared the gospel first with Jews during all of his journeys (Acts 13—14; 16—18; 19—20). Likewise, when imprisoned in Rome, he almost immediately invited the Jewish leaders to listen to Jesus' message (Acts 28:17-23). Acts 17:2 reports that everywhere he went, Paul took the biblical message to the Jewish people first.

Often believers object, "Isn't the phrase 'to the Jew first' a description of the historical spread of the gospel and therefore not a command for us to follow?" If this is true, the use of the phrase in Romans 1:16 proves quite interesting. The past tense would certainly indicate historical description. Yet the verse uses the present tense. Those who pay close attention to "ages" know that we live in the same age as when Paul wrote this. This being the case, a principle true in his time should remain valid today. Further, the same verb governs both phrases, "the power of God" and "to the Jew first." If we assume that "to the Jew first" is purely historical, we must say the same thing about "the power of God."

"But what about Acts 13:46, where Paul says, 'Lo, we turn to the Gentiles,' after the Jews refused to listen? Doesn't this indicate that after the Jewish people rejected the message, it was to go to the Gentiles?" Not quite. Immediately after making this statement, Paul again took the message to Jewish people first (Acts 14:1) and continued this practice everywhere he went (Acts 17:2). Therefore, "to the Jew first" is a matter of principle. God ordered it this way, regardless of whether some particular Jewish people will hear or not, regardless of what happened at one point in history.

God gave a certain order for the spreading of his message. He instructed his people to communicate it to the whole world, but to do this by sharing it with the Jews first. Now, this doesn't mean that Jews are better than Gentiles or have preference over them. God simply decided to establish this order and, after all, some order does need to be followed. And because it is his order, the spreading of the message takes place most effectively when carried out in this way. Two Scripture passages illustrate this principle. Psalm 67:1, "Be merciful to us, and bless us; make your face shine on us ... that your way will be known throughout the earth and your salvation by all nations," describes a situation in which the Jewish people are properly related to God, indicated by "God's blessing" and "his face shining on them." The word that indicates a result. The result of Jews being properly related to God is found in verse 2: the nations of the world will know God's salvation. In other words, if the Jewish people are right with God, the whole world will learn of God's message. Acts 15:16-17 supports this. God will restore Israel to himself so that the whole world will seek him.

Probably because he saw the importance of this order for spreading Jesus' message, Paul made the startling statements in Romans 9:1-5. The Jewish people's salvation meant so much that he wished he could "become unsaved" if that resulted in their salvation. Although this reflects his deep love for his people, it also demonstrates that Paul realized the importance of Israel's salvation in God's purpose.

Several other considerations relate to interpreting the phrase "to the Jew first." If God intended this instruction to be a temporary pattern, we would expect something to indicate its end. But there apparently is no canceling of the instruction. Further, the argument that the Jewish people already heard the message first, and therefore there is no longer any such obligation, proves deceptive. The Gentiles have also heard the gospel and have, by and large, rejected it. Therefore, to be consistent, the historical argument must conclude that the gospel should not be taken to the Gentiles any longer either. Finally, if "to the Jew first" refers only to the historical spreading of Jesus' message, the apostles erred in continuing to share the message with Jewish people first throughout New Testament times. The logical conclusion, then, is that in every generation God's people must communicate his message to the whole world, but in his particular order—to Jews first. We aren't excused because we point to an incident 2000 years ago, when some Jews in some particular city heard the gospel through some particular apostle.

What are the implications of this conclusion? It does not mean that every individual must share the biblical message primarily with Jewish people. But it does mean that the body of the Messiah is responsible for following God's order for spreading his message. Remember, the phrase says "to the Jew first, and *also* to the Gentile," not "and *then* to the Gentile." This indicates priority, not exclusiveness. Because of the Jew's place in God's program to communicate his message, his purpose in the world will be more effectively achieved if done in this order. The salvation of the Jewish people will naturally and inevitably result in the salvation of scores of Gentiles (Ps 67:1-2; Acts 15:16-17; Rom 11:12, 15).

Sound biblical scholars have differed in their understanding of "to the Jew first." The evidence from Scripture seems conclusive to many; however, if this study has left you unconvinced, don't let that get in your way. There are other important reasons for demonstrating a concern for the Jewish people and for communicating God's message to them.

A Debt to Repay

Christians have a debt to repay. After all, the Scriptures have come through the Jewish people. The Bible describes their history and religion, as well as God's revelation to them. Jewish people wrote the entire Old Testament. The whole New Testament, with the possible exception of Luke, was written by Jews.[1] Romans 3:1-2 states it all very clearly: God committed his truths to the Jewish people and decided to use them as the channels of his revelations. Further, Jewish people preserved much of the Bible. They protected it against destruction by its enemies. For example, the Dead Sea community hid its Scripture scrolls in clay jars inside caves so the Romans couldn't destroy them. They guaranteed the accuracy of our existing texts by their painstaking copying methods. Jewish scribes counted the words and letters of the Scripture text by lines and by pages. The total numbers of the words and letters of the copy had to match those of the original. If they did not, the copies were corrected or destroyed if there were too many errors to correct. So Christians should thank the Jewish people for the Bible.

The Savior also came from this people. Jesus was born of a Jewish family and tribe in a Jewish town. He lived as a Jew, followed Jewish religious practices (Gal 4:4) and refused to abolish biblical Judaism (Mt 5:17). Christians owe their Savior to the Jewish people.

Salvation as well came through the Jews (see Rom 11:11-32). The promises of salvation are Jewish. God promised Abraham (and Isaac and Jacob), "In your seed, all nations of the earth will be blessed" (Gen 22:18). According to Galatians 3:8 and Acts 3:25-26, when God said this, he was preaching the gospel to Abraham in the form of a promise. The way of salvation is also Jewish. The Old Testament ceremonies and sacrifices illustrate it. The Old Testament (Lev 1:3-5; 17:11; Is 53:5-6) clearly describes the way of atonement through the exchange-of-life principle (one life given up in place of, in exchange for, another),[2] and the same principle operates today (2 Cor 5:21). Jesus put it simply, "Salvation is of the Jews" (Jn 4:22).

Even the church came from the Jewish people. Its origin and early existence were due to their efforts. Its membership was solely Jewish for the first several years. The synagogue furnished the pattern for the church's structure, practice, worship and administrative system (elders and deacons). The Jewish context provided the concept of apostleship as well. The Hebrew term *shali'ah* described a person authorized and commissioned for a specific responsibility as the representative of another, which is the function of the New Testament apostle. The rabbis described the *shali'ah* as follows: "The one sent by a man is as the man himself."[3] As it expanded, the church's first outreach was conducted by Jews following accepted Jewish practices, and growth resulted.

Finally, Scripture indicates that certain spiritual benefits have come from the Jewish people. Romans 15:27 describes Gentiles as "having been made sharers in the Jews' spiritual things." The Bible elsewhere explains that these spiritual things include enjoying God's promises and blessings, anticipating future glory, and having a relationship with God. All these things have come from the Jewish people, and Gentiles share in these privileges (Eph 2:11-13; 3:4-7; Rom 11:11-18). In fact, Gentiles participate so completely in these things that they are called "the sons of Abraham" (Gal 3:29).

It is apparent that Christians owe much to the Jewish people: the Bible, the Savior, salvation, the church and spiritual benefits. This is a significant debt to repay. Demonstrating a concern for

Jewish people and communicating the biblical message to them helps to repay it.

A Responsibility to Fulfill

Christians should also act this way because they have a specific responsibility. Romans 11:11-15 teaches that God brought salvation to the Gentiles in order to win the Jewish people back to himself. Gentile believers were to provoke the Jews to jealousy, to make them want the atonement available through the Messiah. Have they fulfilled this task? One outstanding evangelical scholar summarized the situation:

> The early Christians were instructed, in their proclamation of the Gospel, to begin at Jerusalem. Both Peter and Paul began with the Jews. But the Christian church has for centuries ... often completely neglected the Jews, and during long periods of time never gotten to Jerusalem at all. This is a tragic and lamentable fact. It is a sin to be confessed and repented of.[4]

Instead of fulfilling their God-given responsibility to the Jews, so-called Christians and Christian nations have persecuted them. Millions of Jewish people have died in Christian countries without ever hearing a clear message about Jesus and atonement. In fact, according to an outstanding conservative leader of the past,

> The attitude of the church to the Jews was almost wilfully aimed to strengthen them in their antipathy to Christianity. The church still owes the Jews the actual proof of Christianity's truth. Is it surprising that the Jewish people are such an insensitive and barren field for the Gospel? The church itself has drenched it it in blood and then heaped stones upon it.[5]

Even today a great number of Jewish people in the United States have not heard a clear presentation of the atonement available through the Messiah.

Consider that Zechariah 13:9 predicts a time ahead when two-thirds of the Jewish people will be killed. They must be told by then. This adds to the already immense responsibility Christians must discharge.

A Spiritual Potential to Develop

Christians must concern themselves for the Jewish people for yet another reason, their great spiritual potential. Many have expressed a growing spiritual hunger and a desire for spiritual vitality. A prominent Jewish lecturer said, "The Jewish nature and soul needs to know God; it must be told about God. Our souls are looking for God and are trying to know God, and no one has told them."

Some Jewish people also expect that shortly God will again act in history. As one rabbi expressed it: "Time is rushing on; God must take a hand in history as he did in the time of Moses. This is the time when Messiah will come. He might even come tomorrow."

At the same time dissatisfaction with traditional Judaism has grown in some quarters. A rabbi evaluated this situation: "We are living in an age where people want something a bit more tangible in their religion. They want to touch, approach, and feel God. Judaism has always been very abstract. . . . [It] raises more questions than it answers. The Jesus movement has all the answers."[6]

This statement, although not necessarily indicating the rabbi's personal beliefs, reflects the growing openness of many Jews to Jesus' message. In fact, in an effort to sound the alarm, another rabbi warned that two to three thousand Jewish people accept Jesus as Messiah every year. Jewish people have not, by and large, rejected the Messiah. Many have no concept of Messiah and know little about the Old Testament. They haven't really received a true picture of Jesus. Many are open to this message if it is presented properly. The potential is there.

A Strategic Time

We live in a strategic and exciting time. This should sharpen concern for the Jewish people and interest in communicating the biblical message to them. Our generation has seen prophecy fulfilled before our eyes. Israel was restored to the Jewish people in our time, just as Scripture predicted (see, for example, Is 11:11-12). Jerusalem, the most holy city of the Jews, finally returned to Jewish hands after 1900 years of foreign domination. This too, just as Scripture predicted (Lk 21:24). The nations of the world are taking sides in a pattern that fits prophetic descriptions (Ezek 28, Dan 11). The events in our physical environment are beginning to match up with the signs Jesus gave of his return (Mt 24). Remember, too, in that last great time period before Jesus rules the earth, the Jewish people will be God's greatest spiritual task force in history (Rev 7). You can set the stage for these great events by sharing God's message with a people open to it at a most strategic and exciting time in history.

So there are many important reasons to be actively concerned for the Jewish people and to communicate the biblical message to them. God has given a command to obey, a debt to repay, a responsibility to discharge, and a tremendous potential to cultivate at a most strategic and exciting time. Can you expect a good response? Yes, if you communicate properly.

2

THE JEWISH PEOPLE IN THE PROGRAM OF GOD

In all communication the communicator (the source) needs to understand the person with whom he is communicating (the respondent). Without such understanding, communication frequently breaks down because the lack of common experiences between the source and respondent obstructs the process. Respondents interpret messages based on their prior experiences and on their view of the world. But these may differ radically from those of the source. So the respondent may understand a message very differently from the way intended by the source. Therefore, the source must carefully phrase his message in terms of the respondent's experiences and understanding if he is to communicate accurately and effectively. This in turn means that the source must develop a sensitivity to the background, culture, experiences and frame of reference that the respondent brings into a conversation. (This is part of what 1 Corinthians 9:19-23 means.) The next several chapters will survey areas essential to achieving the sensitivity necessary for good communication with Jewish people.

One area vital for a proper understanding of the Jewish people includes their history and destiny, particularly God's purposes for them. The Bible contains the outlines of this. Genesis 1—11 is very striking. It condenses a great many events covering a long period of time into several chapters. For example, these chapters say little about such outstanding events as creation and the flood, events about which many long to know more. God seems to say, "This is not the main point; these are not the most important things for you to know." He rushes through these events to something more significant, found in chapter 12. Chapters 1—11 cover a long, indeterminate period, whereas chapters 12—50 cover only about 200 years! God definitely emphasizes this latter section, and chapter 12 stands as the turning point.

God's Purpose for Our World: Abrahamic Contract

In this chapter God chooses Abraham and makes several important promises to him. These promises contain, in seed form, the basics of God's purpose for our world.[1] The promises, and their later expansions, are often called the Abrahamic Covenant or Contract. By understanding the terms of the contract, we can better understand God's actions through the rest of Scripture and in the history of the world—past, present and future. Verses 1-7 contain three key terms which unlock God's purpose: *land* (vv. 1, 7), *nation* or its synonym *seed* (v. 2), and *blessing* (vv. 2-3). God promises to give Abraham and his descendants the land of Canaan. He promises to multiply them and make them a great nation. Finally, God promises to make them his instrument for blessing the world. He then describes these promises in three ways.

Genesis 13:14-18 contains the first two ways. In verse 15 God says to Abraham, "All the land which you see I will give to you and your descendants *for ever*" (compare 17:7-8). The text clearly states that God's contract with Abraham is a "forever" contract; it is *eternal*. The second way God describes the contract arises from verses 14-17. God tells Abraham to look around at the land he would give him, and then to walk through it. The land Abraham saw, the ground he walked on, was real land, a definite piece of geography. God wasn't using metaphorical or symbolic language.

In chapter 15:3-5 God tells Abraham that his seed (descendants) would originate from his own body and then multiply greatly. His seed would not be something merely metaphorical or symbolic; they would be real, physical children and grandchildren descended directly from him. As a result Abraham expected a real piece of geography and descendants coming from his own body. So God's promises to Abraham were *literal*, not symbolic.

The third important way God describes the contract comes out in chapter 15:7-18. God instructs Abraham to prepare the items used in ratifying Near Eastern contracts at that time. Abraham takes certain animals, cuts them in half and separates the halves. The contracting parties would then walk between the halves to ratify the agreement. So Abraham thought he and God would do this. However, verses 17-18 show that only God walked between the halves, not Abraham. By doing this God indicated that he alone was responsible for the terms of the contract. The contract's fulfillment depended on him, not Abraham. It was not conditioned on Abraham's follow-through or his descendants' actions. It was *unconditional*, depending solely on God's promise and commitment to carry it out (see Gal 3:17-18).

So the Abrahamic contract includes the land, a seed and great blessing, and the Bible describes these promises as eternal, literal and unconditional. God then confirms the contract with Abraham's son Isaac (Gen 17:19) and later with Isaac's son Jacob and his descendants (Gen 28:13-14). Jacob's descendants became the nation of Israel, the Jewish people. The land of Canaan which God gave to Abraham and the Jewish people has been known historically as Israel or Palestine (its borders are described in Genesis 15:18). The Abrahamic contract, then, guarantees the permanent national existence of the Jewish people, their perpetual title to the land of Israel, and the certainty of God's blessing on them and ultimately on the whole world through them. The rest of Scripture and history unfolds this contract and shows how God works out his purpose for our world.

God had promised to create a nation out of Abraham. Several things were essential for this: a people, a government and a homeland. Genesis 12—24 relates the story of the man God chose, Abraham. In chapters 25—45 God selects the people, i.e., which of

Abraham's descendants he would work through, and then tells the story of their lives. He specifies the promised line of Abraham as going through Isaac and Jacob. Genesis 46 to Exodus 18 recounts how God preserved the people he chose. Instead of following instructions to be a blessing to those around them, Jacob's family was, as Jacob put it, "a stench" (Gen 34:30). So God took them to Egypt to discipline them. But the time in Egypt also preserved them as a people. They had intermingled with the Canaanites (Gen 38:2) and so were in danger of losing their distinctiveness and purpose. However, the Egyptians were separatists who opposed intermarriage, so Jacob's family preserved their identity. In Egypt the family multiplied sufficiently to become a nation (about two million people left Egypt under Moses), which God preserved miraculously through Egyptian oppression and through the wanderings in the desert.

A Nation in Its Land: Mosaic Contract

God provided the first essential for nationhood, a people. When the people arrived at Mt. Sinai, he gave them the second essential. He provided a constitution for the nation (Ex 19—Lev 27, and the entire book of Deuteronomy), thus establishing its government, in the covenant communicated through Moses. The literary form of the Mosaic covenant resembled that of the international treaties of the time. It was in the form of a treaty between a servant nation and a great king. God, the great King, graciously specified for Israel, the servant nation, the conditions for living under his rule. These explained the details of living the totality of their lives before him. Since God was sovereign over every area of life, there could be no distinction between sacred and secular. This was a true theocracy. Its constitution contained principles of conducting governmental as well as social, family and personal affairs; principles of maintaining and expressing a proper relationship with God (not of entering such a relationship, which they had already done) although surrounded by a godless society; and promises and warnings concerning their stay in the land.

God expected Israel to be a kingdom of priests (Ex 19:5-6), acting as a "lighthouse" and bringing others to himself. To do this, they had to be holy, the root idea of which means "set apart" or "distinct." This kind of holiness or distinctness comes when people obey God. The people of Israel were to live God's way, so that others would be attracted to him by their distinctiveness (Deut 4:5-10).

God promised that if the people kept the guidelines of the Mosaic contract, they would experience his blessings, be a blessing to others, fulfill their calling and enjoy life in the land. However, if they did not, the results would be automatic (Deut 11:26-28). Deuteronomy mentions these blessings and results. Chapter 28 predicts Israel's disobedience and the resulting discipline of God which culminated in their dispersion. Chapter 30 predicts God's bringing them back into the land of Israel as part of their final restoration to him.

The contract tells the people how to live properly before God so as to enjoy life in the land, what will happen if they do not, and God's subsequent program for the Jewish people with respect to the land. Therefore, the Mosaic contract expands the Abrahamic contract's *land* promises.

After receiving their constitution and government, the only essential remaining for nationhood was the possession of the homeland. The book of Joshua records God's giving Israel the land he promised. God had now completed his creation of a nation. He had prepared it both to be and to receive a blessing.

Israel next moves into the time of the judges (Judg 1—1 Sam 11). Anarchy and turning from God characterized this period. People "did their own thing," whatever they felt was right (Judg 21:25). They forgot about God and what he had done (Judg 2:10ff.). The result, as God had warned them in Deuteronomy, was oppression from outside and corruption inside the nation. Even when he raised up judges to liberate them and the people finally turned back to God, they quickly turned away again. At the end of this period they asked for a king, and God gave them their wish.

Inconsistency characterized the time of the kings (1 Sam 12— Zeph 3, excluding Ezra, Nehemiah, Esther, Ezekiel and Daniel). The king's leadership and example were crucial. If he remained faithful to God, the nation worshiped and obeyed God. If the king turned away from God, the nation did too. Unfortunately, most kings turned their backs on God and led Israel down a miserable road. David came the closest to being an ideal king; it was with him that God ratified another important contract.

The Promised Seed: Davidic Contract

The primary passages dealing with this contract are 2 Samuel 7:5-16 and Psalm 89:1-37. They expand the Abrahamic contract's *seed* promises. The Davidic contract describes Abraham's greatest seed, Messiah, as the one who will reign over the earth with Israel —the rest of Abraham's seed—as the center of his rule.

David wanted to build a house (temple) for God. God refused to allow this and used the occasion to make some great promises to David. Some concerned David's son Solomon, who would build a house for God. Others went far beyond Solomon. God promised to build an eternal house for David. Near Eastern cultures often used the image of a house to indicate a line of descendants. So God here guarantees that David's seed will never be completely wiped out. Next he promised to establish David's throne forever. *Throne* signifies the authority to rule. In other words, the authority to rule Israel would always belong to David and his descendants. His family would never be displaced by another as the rightful royal line. God also guaranteed the existence of David's kingdom forever. *Kingdom* implies a domain, the physical place of a reign over existing people. So God promises that a kingdom will always exist over which David's line will rule, a kingdom which will have Israel at its center. Thus the Davidic contract, like the contracts before it, guarantees Israel's ultimate, continued existence.

There was a condition attached to part of the contract. Disobedience on the part of David's descendants would result in God's judgment (2 Sam 7:14-15; Ps 89:30-34); the disobedient would not participate in the promised blessings. They might also lose their part in ruling Israel. They would not experience the blessings because they would not appropriate them by faith. However, disobedience would not set aside the covenant (Ps 89:30-34). David's seed would remain the royal line. Changing forms of government or divine judgment might interrupt the actual rule over the kingdom by David's line. But, the line, the right to the throne and the royal domain *would be preserved and never lost,* and this despite sin, captivity, intrigue or dispersion. The attempt by Queen Athaliah to exterminate the royal line and the survival of Joash (2 Kings

11) provides a good example of this preservation.

Therefore, continuous political government did not need to exist, but the line with its rights had to be preserved and ultimately restored. Thus, the Messiah's rule over Israel on David's throne is founded on the Davidic contract. And based on this contract, the prophets expected Messiah, as David's greatest descendant and Abraham's promised seed, to restore David's kingdom and reign over Israel in millennial blessings (Jer 23:5-6). David's line was preserved and eventually culminated in the Messiah. It will yet be restored in all its fullness.

The prophets (Is 1—Mal 4) functioned during the time of the kings and afterward. They acted as prosecuting attorneys; i.e., they indicted the nation for its disobedience. Their books read almost like courtroom scenes. They also preached the covenants. The Mosaic covenant had promised blessings for obedience and judgment for disobedience, so the prophets had nothing but judgment to offer the nation for their disobedience. Yet their messages end with hope because the Abrahamic and Davidic covenants promised that God would use Israel to bless the world and be the center of Messiah's reign. As they surveyed the situation, this wasn't happening. But God had promised it would. Therefore it still had to happen, and they looked forward to this. As part of this anticipation, and through the context of the prophets, God revealed the New Covenant.

The Culmination of the Blessing Program: New Contract

The new contract (Jer 31:30-39; Ezek 36:22-32) expands the Abrahamic contract's blessing promises and shows how Israel will be a source of blessing for all the world. The contract's terms, made specifically with Israel (Jer 30:31), are spiritually radical. God promises to wipe out sin. He promises to give believers a new nature with new drives to obey him and keep his guidelines. He will put his Spirit in believers to energize the new nature. He will establish an intimate relationship with man, eventually with all humanity. These tremendous blessings ultimately relate to Israel's restoration and the benefits of Messiah's reign (Jer 31:37-39). Then, the whole world will share in this. However, individuals can enter into many of these blessings today by means of spiritual birth

(Ezek 36:25-27; see also Jn 3:5, 7, 10).

Jesus identified himself as the new covenant's mediator or ratifier (Lk 22:19-20; Heb 9:15). He made it possible for it to go into effect and for people to enjoy its benefits. The Holy Spirit's dramatic coming at Pentecost, then, signaled the new contract's initiation. God there indicated that he had put his Spirit in believers as promised in the contract (Ezek 36:24-27). Its other terms, as well as the unfulfilled promises of the other covenants, await a future fulfillment.

The Old Testament's last statements (Mal 3:22-24, or 4:4-6) underline the centrality of these contracts. The prophet tells God's people to follow the Mosaic covenant's guidelines as the way of life that pleases God. He then alerts them to look for the coming of Elijah, the forerunner of Messiah, Messiah who fulfills the Abrahamic, Mosaic and Davidic contracts and institutes the new contract.

The New Testament carries on the flow of the covenants. Matthew, for example, introduces Jesus as the son of Abraham and David (Mt 1:1), a theme followed throughout the Gospel to show that he fulfilled these contracts. In the Sermon on the Mount Jesus presents himself as the Mosaic covenant's fulfillment as well (Mt 5:17). Prior to his birth, the angel who visited Mary announced that Jesus would be given his father David's throne (Lk 1:32). This indicated his close relationship to the Davidic contract again. Mary, in her response (Lk 1:54-55), expresses gratitude to God for helping his servant Israel in keeping with his promises to Abraham. She understood the Messiah's unique relation to the Abrahamic covenant as its source of blessing. Zacharias, John the Baptizer's father, continues the theme by referring to Jesus as the Savior from David's house and the fulfillment of promises to Abraham (Lk 1:68-79). In a magnificent way Hebrews highlights Jesus as the Mosaic contract's fulfillment and the new contract's mediator.

Both Old and New Testaments make the significance of the covenants quite clear, then. By studying the Abrahamic contract, and the Mosaic, Davidic and new contracts' elaboration of it, we get a picture of God's purposes in our world and Israel's place in his program. Some of his promises to Israel have been fulfilled. Others await a future fullfillment as God continues to work with his people through history.

3

ASPECTS OF THE JEWISH WORLD VIEW

An essential part of good communication involves understanding the respondent, the person being addressed. Because the respondent interprets messages in terms of his experiences and his understanding of reality (his world view), a good communicator must have some grasp of the elements that make up the respondent's world view. The study of the basic aspects of a Jewish world view makes for an involved but intriguing adventure. Any attempt to summarize them in a single chapter, while beneficial, can only be suggestive and elementary at best. One important preliminary consideration deserves mention. The Jewish people and their world view are not monolithic or homogeneous, so the best that one can hope for is to describe some general trends.[1]

Religious Thought: Unity amidst Diversity
The phrase *unity amidst diversity* best characterizes the first aspect of the Jewish world view, religious thought. Consider two

preliminary observations. First, a trend exists today to present Judaism in terms of the contemporary world, to demonstrate its relevance to modern life. Questioning is part of this trend, as it has been throughout Jewish history. Even the Talmud (the authoritative multivolume traditional commentary on the Old Testament, put in written form A.D. 200-500) demonstrates the importance of questioning. Its authors structured it in the form of a discussion of religious questions. Among Jewish youth today the questioning has developed along two quite different paths. One path questions what the older generation is putting aside by way of traditions. The other questions the meaning or relevance of the traditions. Some Jewish youth are becoming more religiously devout, while others are putting the traditions aside. But this very questioning and drive for relevance have made Judaism a dynamic religion.

Second, most Jewish people have a strong historical orientation. As a result even the less traditional have a respect for tradition, although it varies from person to person. The varying levels of respect expressed by the three daughters in *Fiddler on the Roof* illustrate this well.

Several important unifying elements are common to much of Jewish religious thinking. The unity of God—the belief that God is only one person—stands as the most important. Most Jews view the *Shema* (Deut 6:4), chanted weekly in the synagogues, as the basic statement of this. Further, God is a *moral* deity; he bases his relationships with people on what is right and wrong.

A second unifying element is the idea of the Jewish people's "chosenness." In Jewish thinking this means that God has revealed his essence to mankind through the Jewish people (see Rom 3:1-2). This involves not only a privilege but also a responsibility, to clearly reveal God's essence to others.

"Morality is more important than ceremony" is the third element. A good, ethical life is more valuable than observing the religious practices, and action is more important than belief. The Talmud indicates that the first question God asks of the departed soul when it reaches his tribunal is not "Did you fast on Yom Kippur, keep Sabbath or follow the customs?" but "Were you honest in business?"

The fourth element rejects both indulgence and asceticism. Judaism aims for a balance. "You shall rejoice before the Lord in study, worship and good deeds, but also in food, drink, clothes and fellowship."[2] So it strongly emphasizes life and living, the full enjoyment of life and creation as God intended.

Although unity characterizes Jewish religious thought, diversity also exists within the family of Judaism. The various branches or systems of religious practice reflect this. The Orthodox tend to adhere strictly to religious tradition and Jewish law. Conservative Judaism affirms the Jewish law's authority and seeks to conserve tradition but allows for its adaptation to modern society. Reform Judaism rejects final authority and form and therefore accepts as binding only those aspects of the traditional codes that are "relevant and elevating" to modern man's life. Reconstructionism believes Judaism must reconstruct itself to meet today's world conditions by integrating Judaism with naturalistic philosophy. Judaism, according to Reconstructionists, is therefore the evolving religious civilization of the Jewish people, to be thought of in natural, not supernatural, terms. Beyond these religious expressions exists a large group of Jewish people who are religiously unaffiliated, secular, agnostic or atheistic.

A Survey of Jewish Theology

Due to this diversity it is difficult to describe definitive areas of Jewish theology. Yet a basic survey can help. Judaism, properly understood, does not consist of the drudgery of slavishly observing minute laws and practices. It involves life in the presence of the God of creation. Life comes from God; what he made is good and should be enjoyed. God's creation is a good place to live, a place to enjoy, but also a place where man has certain responsibilities. These involve a life of obedience to God, but this makes possible the enjoyment of life in all its fullness. God intended man to be a whole person, reaching and using his full capacities—emotional, physical, mental, social and spiritual. Then not only can he live a life that satisfies him, but he also becomes part of a community of people and demonstrates concern for others. The Law then becomes a series of opportunities to choose and take advantage of, an invitation by God to walk with him. The holiday *Simchat Torah* ("rejoicing in the Law") illustrates this. Jewish people dance, sing and celebrate that God gave them his laws. The Law is a crown, a privilege, a blessing (see Ps 119:1, 2, 24, 94, 103, 111, 127-130; Rom 7:12).

God's indivisible unity stands as the cornerstone of Jewish theology. His absolute oneness is an unchanging fundamental principle. He is also completely spiritual, impossible to imagine in human form. As Maimonides, an important medieval Jewish leader, expressed it, "The Creator, blessed be his name, has no bodily form, and no form can represent him." God transcends the physical. He is not a God solely of justice and wrath, but a God of great love and mercy. One of the regular synagogue readings expresses this: "Thou, O Lord, art a God full of compassion and gracious; slow to anger and plenteous in mercy and truth" (Ps 86:15).

Jewish theology does not view man as totally depraved and under the curse of original sin, but rather emphasizes the human possibility of doing good. While it is definitely aware of man's evil inclinations and sin, it applies itself primarily to the challenge of helping man face up to and overcome his specific faults. Neither beliefs nor ceremonies, although instructive and beneficial, suffice for this. Fulfilling the commands of God (good deeds, or *mitzvot*) is the essential thing. The ethical life based on the Law overcomes sin and evil.

When man's shortcomings prevent him from consistently living the proper ethical life, repentance becomes necessary. "Repentance is the remedy offered by the Holy One, blessed be he."[3] This involves a decision to return to God's laws and abandon evil deeds and intentions. Two other things are essential for man to live in proper relationship with God: prayer and the study of Torah (the Law). Concerning the latter the Talmud says, "The first question that is put to a man on the day of Judgment is, 'Have you busied yourself with the study of Torah?' " (*Sanhedrin* 7a, *Yoma* 35b). Although some disagree, Jewish theology generally holds that death is not the end of life. Man lives on in other realms. However, the actual nature of the world to come remains basically unknown. God will ultimately resolve that question.

Jewish people generally differ over their ideas of the Messiah. The more traditional pray for his coming and believe the world's redemption awaits this. The Messiah will be a mysterious "super-man" or a great, gifted leader who will purge the world of evil and will establish a worldwide system of peace, justice and the knowledge of God. However, he will not come until the Jewish people fulfill their function as Jews by observing God's Law and serving as moral examples to remind the world of God's teachings. Less traditional Jews have no concept of Messiah or else think in terms of a Messianic age, a golden age yet to come. Therefore, man becomes responsible for bringing in this age of peace, justice and the knowledge of God.

Cultural Aspects of Judaism
Part of the Jewish world view is its perspective on education. For many, the search for wisdom surpasses other things as man's noblest activity. A traditional saying bears this out: "Learning takes precedence over all things." Almost nothing characterizes Jewishness more than its emphasis on learning. Some Jews view study as a holy activity, its very act as a prayer to God. A traditional view of heaven reflects this: "sitting eternally with others and studying in a college on high." Although most Jewish study was once religious, thus explaining this attitude, the respect for study has carried over into nonreligious areas as well.

Another aspect of Jewish culture involves social values, which are frequently rooted in religious values. One value focuses on the concept of *kedushah* (holiness, sanctity, right living). This quality is related to God's holiness and is what God seeks to find in man. Further, man's actions show it to be part of God's nature. In other words, a Jew should live in such a way that others will regard God as holy. Therefore, to mistreat your fellow man not only destroys your own reputation but God's as well. You have failed to testify truly to the nature of God.

Another of the social values revolves around *mitzvah*, the commands of God, and the conduct based on these commands. Since conduct most accurately demonstrates a relationship with God, *mitzvah* describes those patterns of conduct, based on God's nature and commands, which testify truly to the nature of God. Most of these patterns express themselves in the social realm.

The "slaves in Egypt" motif, as a basis for values, also relates directly to the social realm. The religious writings urge Jews to remember that they were once slaves in Egypt. At Passover a familiar phrase reminds them, "Because they did it to me in Egypt, I must learn not to do it to others." So Jewish people are taught to be considerate of others and be sensitive to their needs.

Related to this is the conviction that God's image exists in every man. This should condition man's attitudes toward others. Because God's image resides in man, man must be concerned about social justice, about the dispossessed, the weak, the stranger, the little guy. Callousness and indifference toward suffering are not options. Further, concern must be expressed in concrete action—involvement with people and causes, demonstrations, political activism.

The vision of the good society and the conviction that history has meaning form another basis for social values. History is moving toward a goal, the golden age of perfection in the future, a goal which should become the focus and pattern for man's efforts. Peace and social justice characterize this age. God expects man not only to anticipate its arrival but to work toward its accomplishment.

Another important part of the Jewish world view centers on the home. From the very beginning, Jewish people have had a strong emphasis on the family. It has been central to the ongoing of the community. Jewish people have been forced to be quite mobile throughout history, so a close-knit family life helped to provide roots. Into this close-knit family life has been incorporated a whole set of religious ceremonies transforming the family into a little sanctuary. During the Sabbath meal and the holidays father and mother presides much like priest and priestess. On the Sabbath the family eats hallah (a kind of bread) with salt, reminiscent of the Levitical meal offerings. This elevates the act of eating to the level of an offering to God. Similarly, many other things in the traditional Jewish family take on a religious significance, serving as continual reminders of life under God. For example, the mezuzah (a small cylinder containing portions of Deuteronomy attached to the door frame) reminds the family of its obligations before God and of God's presence and protection.

The Jewish home not only stands at the heart of Jewish faith but also serves as the training ground for life. Here, as part of their sacred duty, parents prepare their children for life (see Deut 4: 5-10; 6:4-9). In the home the children develop maturity that will give them, in turn, a good home and marriage, a loving union of two human beings helping each other find joy and fulfillment.

To adequately understand the Jewish frame of reference, one must understand the role of the Jewish community and the place of community involvement. Jewishness is more than a religion or race. The Jews of the world form a people held together not only by ties of a distinctive religion but also by a common history, culture, social experience and destiny. They form a true community, one occasionally described as one big family. Over forty per cent of this world community live in the United States. Of these, approximately two-thirds reside in seven large cities: New York, Los Angeles, Philadelphia, Chicago, Miami, Boston and Washington, D.C.

The Jewish person fulfills the requirements for being a member of the community in good standing by demonstrating his loyalty to and identification with the Jewish people. The community structure allows for this in three arenas: synagogue, Jewish agencies and Jewish causes. Involvement in one or more of these areas makes for credible Jewishness.

The synagogue serves as the center of not only religious life but adult education and social action programs as well, so a person can participate in the synagogue without being religious.

People can associate with any of a large variety of Jewish agencies. These include a broad spectrum of service, fraternal, social welfare and community relations organizations such as B'nai B'rith, Hadassah, American Zionist Organization, American Jewish Committee and United Jewish Appeal. People can also participate in educational centers such as Jewish schools and community centers. A community center provides an important community meeting place and functions as an educational body, health club, social agency, civic center and recreation place combined.

Involvement in Jewish causes is a vital way to demonstrate solidarity within the local community and with other communities worldwide. Causes can take the form of marches, demonstrations, fund-raisers, relief, financial assistance, political pressure, and so on.

Major Jewish Concerns

Several major concerns have surfaced within the Jewish community, some of which we will discuss in greater detail in later chapters. One such concern relates to the problems of assimilation and
Jewish survival. The term *assimilation* describes the tendency on
the part of some Jews to drop out of the Jewish community and become so thoroughly associated with the rest of society that they are
unrecognizable as Jews and for all practical purposes don't regard
themselves as such. Two factors make up assimilation: an objective
factor, a loss of distinctiveness; and a subjective factor, a loss of
the feeling of identity. Some have suggested that by the century's
end there will be only two million self-proclaimed Jews in the
United States.[4] In other words, almost four million Jewish people
will assimilate. Jewish leaders view two things as the major cul-
prits in assimilation—conversion and intermarriage—and direct
much effort to combat the problem. In recent years the increasing
importance attached to Jewish survival, in a sense the converse of
assimilation, has spurred the efforts against assimilation. Jewish
survival implies not only their viable existence as a distinguish-
able entity worldwide but also Israel's security and survival.

Another concern revolves around the oppression of Jewish
minorities worldwide. The situation of the Jews in the Soviet
Union forms the focal point of much of the concern. Jewish people
there have repeatedly suffered persecution, repression and discrimination. They have no freedom to worship, protests are stifled,
people are jailed or lose their jobs, and emigration is severely restricted. Recent reports out of the Soviet Union have demonstrated
that the situation has deteriorated rather than improved. Since
1976 the Kremlin's sanctioning of a policy equating Zionism with
racism has produced increased harassment of Jews seeking to emi-
grate, so much so that for every twenty-five people allowed to
leave each year during the early 1970s, only one was allowed to go
in 1982. The Jewish community in Syria fares no better. They suffer
under severe restrictions and undergo periodic persecution and
torture. Jewish minorities in other Arab and Eastern European
countries face similar problems.

A third concern is anti-Semitism. It consists of an irrational anti-
Jewish sentiment which often leads to discrimination and vio-

lence. Many times it includes the tendency to see Jewish people in the roles of rival, outsider and scapegoat. Many Jews feel anti-Semitism is increasing in the United States and abroad. Due to the organized church's strong historical connection with anti-Semitic acts, Jewish people often view Christianity as a major contributing force to anti-Semitism. The Holocaust—the Nazi program to exterminate the Jewish people which killed six million Jews during World War II—stands as anti-Semitism's historical epitome. Jews view Christians, apart from a few notable exceptions, as not having opposed Nazi efforts and in many cases as having supported them. For example, so-called Christian nations refused entry to Jewish people fleeing Nazi persecution and returned them to their occupied nations. It appears that political and economic expediency had greater value than Jewish lives. The oil crises of the 1970s and the resulting petro-diplomacy have indicated a return to these same values.

The fourth concern focuses on Zionism and the State of Israel. Zionism is the movement which seeks to respond to the Jewish problems of dispersion, oppression and the threat of annihilation by establishing a Jewish national home in a Jewish state. It represents the national liberation movement of the Jewish people. It has several objectives: to establish a homeland for Jews, to safeguard this homeland and to make it a place where alienated Jews from all over the world can come and be freely Jewish. Although Zionism flows in nearly every Jewish person's bloodstream, it is not a homogeneous movement. It represents a spirit which has taken various organizational and nonorganizational forms, both religious and secular. Occasionally, extreme forms held by a minority appear but are repudiated by the majority.

There are other important aspects of the Jewish world view and culture. For further study, reference should be made to works which treat such subjects in depth.

4

A SURVEY OF CHURCH-SYNAGOGUE RELATIONS

A Historical Overview

A proper understanding of Jewish people, and especially their reaction to things Christian, implies at least a summary knowledge of the history of contacts between the church and the Jewish people. Although some of the trends in these contacts had their roots earlier, the fourth century, when Constantine made Christianity the Roman Empire's official religion, provides a convenient starting point for this very brief survey. In officially recognizing Christianity, Constantine also began enacting restrictions against the Jewish people. These laws soon became more and more oppressive and inclusive. For example, Christians could not be circumcised, thus effectively ending any conversions to Judaism and any potential proselytizing by Jewish people. If either Christians or Jews disobeyed, they would be exiled and their property confiscated. Christians and Jews could not intermarry because that was considered fornication. The government impounded money sent to

Palestine and to the Jewish people. The laws barred Jews from public office. In many places laws did not allow Jews to celebrate Sabbath or Passover.

This anti-Jewish attitude was not solely political but religious as well. John Chrysostom, a fourth-century church leader and committed follower of Jesus, wrote concerning the Jewish people:

[They are] inveterate murderers, destroyers, men possessed by the devil. . . . Debauchery and drunkenness have given them the manners of the pig and the lusty goat. They know only one thing, to satisfy their gullets, get drunk, to kill and maim one another. . . . They have surpassed the ferocity of wild beasts, for they murder their offspring and immolate them to the devil. . . . The Jewish disease must be guarded against. . . . The Christian's duty is to hate the Jews.[1]

Medieval times merely intensified these attitudes. The Crusades provide a good example. The Crusaders intended to free the Holy Land from the infidel invaders. On the way they passed through numerous Jewish villages. A typical scene in the villages included rounding up the Jewish people, herding them into the synagogue and then burning it to the ground with men, women and children inside. This was done, for example, in Jerusalem in 1099. Various Crusader armies massacred tens of thousands of Jews on their marches.

Certainly the Jewish people's plight should have improved with the enlightment brought about by the Scholastics. But this was not to be. Witness the words of Thomas Aquinas: "The Jew is nothing more than an animal or servant. . . . It would be licit, according to custom, to hold Jews . . . in perpetual servitude, and therefore princes may regard their possessions as belonging to the state."[2]

The situation worsened once more during the Inquisition years. Forced baptisms, confiscation of property, torture and burning at the stake characterized this period for the Jewish people. As a result 50,000 died.

The period culminated in the sudden expulsion of the entire Spanish Jewish population numbering about 300,000. The Spanish Jewish culture was one of the richest of its day, and Jews had lived there peacefully until this time. As they left Spain and her colonies, they little realized that starvation, enslavement, shipwreck and death would face many of them before their hard journey ended.

One would expect the Reformation to ease the anti-Jewish attitudes, and to some extent it did. However, much anti-Semitism continued even in the Reformers' writings. Luther, after earlier being sympathetic to the Jewish people, charged them with being poisoners, ritual murderers and parasites. He advocated their expulsion from Germany and destruction of their synagogues and books, writing, "The Jews are brutes, their synagogues are pigsties; they ought to be burned.... They live by evil and plunder; they are wicked beasts that ought to be driven out like mad dogs."[3]

Calvin did little better, calling Jews "profane, barking dogs, as stupid as cattle, a confounded rabble."[4] Statements like these, made by virtually all the Reformers, brought about the actions suggested.

Moving into modern times we see new forms of anti-Semitism developing and others continuing. The early part of this century witnessed the appearance of *The Protocols of the Elders of Zion.* The *Protocols* claimed to give evidence about a Jewish conspiracy intent on conquering the world and asserted that Jews were the monetary powers behind world governments. From these powerful positions they set nations against each other to achieve their devious ends. A London correspondent exposed this in 1921 as a fabrication done in Czarist Russia and associated with the Russian Orthodox Church. It was plagiarized from a French novel and a German adventure story. Unfortunately, the *Protocols* never received a proper burial and have been repeatedly resurrected even in recent books.[5] The noted essayist and historian Hilaire Belloc was just one of many who helped further the intent of the *Protocols.* "We must not judge the Jews according to our ideas.... It is undeniable that every Jew betrays his employer.... The Jews cannot betray any country, for they do not possess one.... The Jew regards every country ... as a place where he may find some profit for himself."[6]

Those who wrote and those who believed these things were intelligent, educated and usually religious men from "Christian" countries.

The Holocaust perpetrated by Hitler and Nazi Germany looms as

history's greatest anti-Jewish atrocity. Before it ended, the Holocaust brutally exterminated six million Jewish men, women and
children, genocide beyond description and unparalleled in human
history. Apart from some notable exceptions, the virtual silence of
the Christian community, and in many cases its acquiescence or
support, during these events has shocked many thoughtful people.
More disturbing yet, as a study of Mein Kampf reveals, Hitler
viewed himself as fulfilling Luther's teaching concerning the Jews.

He believed himself to be the savior who would bring redemption to the German people through the annihilation of the Jews,
that people who embodied in his eyes, the satanic hosts. When
he wrote or spoke about his holy mission, he used words . . . like
"consecration," "salvation," "redemption," "resurrection,"
"God's will." The murder of the Jews, in his fantasies, was commanded by divine providence and he was the chosen instrument
for that task. He referred frequently to his "mission," but no-
where near so explicitly as in Mein Kampf: "Hence today I believe I am acting in accordance with the will of the Almighty
Creator: by defending myself against the Jew I am fighting for
the work of the Lord."[7]
The teaching given grade-school students reflects similar attitudes, as this quote from a third-grade text attests: "Just as Jesus redeemed mankind from sin and hell, so did Hitler rescue the German people from destruction."[8]

Hitler further emphasized his connections with the church at a
1933 meeting with church officials, where he declared that he
"merely wanted to do more effectively what the church had attempted to accomplish for so long," maintaining that his actions
were service to a common cause. In fact, the sign greeting Jews at
Dachau, one of the most infamous of the Nazi death camps, read:
"You are here because you killed our God." Thus Jewish people
tend to view the Holocaust as one of their historical contacts with
the church.

The statements of Franz Delitzsch, an outstanding evangelical
of the past, accurately summarize the history of contacts between
the church—both unbelievers and committed followers of Jesus—
and the synagogue.

The attitude of the Church to the Jews was almost willfully aimed to strengthen them in their antipathy to Christianity. The Church still owes the Jews the actual proof of Christianity's truth. Is it surprising that the Jewish people are such an insensitive and barren field for the Gospel? The Church itself has drenched it in blood and then heaped stones upon it.[9]

The Modern Perspective

But all this is past; what about the present? Surely in today's educated, civilized society no one gets involved in such things. Several examples should provide an adequate response. Over the last fifteen years the Soviet Union alone has published and distributed over a hundred anti-Semitic books and brochures, with editions frequently numbering 150,000 to 200,000 copies each. These are not restricted to domestic use but are widely exported to Arab, African and Third World countries and are often featured in publications of the PLO (Palestine Liberation Organization).[10]

A wave of anti-Semitism has swept through Latin America since the summer of 1982, fanned by the media. Jewish people there live in fear, often with their suitcases packed. Anti-Semitic slogans have been plastered on synagogues and at crossroads. Death threats and bomb threats have been received. In Colombia a pro-PLO demonstration ended with cries of "Death to the Jews!"Anti-Semitic cartoons and statements have appeared in major newspapers in Mexico and Venezuela. And the situation is similar elsewhere in Latin America. Since 1976 there has been a disturbing rise in anti-Semitism and a re-emergence of Nazi tactics and thinking in Argentina, where people are jailed, tortured and sexually abused simply because they are Jews.[11]

Increased anti-Semitism has afflicted Western Europe as well. In 1979 during the solemn memorial of Kristallnacht (the initial outbreak of violence against German Jews in 1939), numerous slogans appeared publicly: "The Fuehrer lives!" "Jews out!" "A dead Jew is a good Jew!"[12] On October 3, 1980, a French synagogue was bombed during a holiday observance. About the same time, a bar mitzvah celebration was bombed in West Germany. In August 1982 two gunmen threw a hand grenade into a crowded Jewish restaurant in Paris and then sprayed gunfire in all directions. Six people died and twenty-two were injured, bringing the death toll from such incidents in France to eighteen in seven months. In October 1982 a crowd of Jews leaving holiday celebrations at Rome's main synagogue were met by grenades and a hail of machine gunfire. The attackers killed a two-year-old boy and wounded thirty-four others. Not isolated incidents, these events are part of a rising tide of attacks on Jews across Western Europe, indicating the reappearance of Europe's traditional anti-Semitism.[13]

The United States has not escaped the problem. "For the third straight year, reported acts of anti-Semitism doubled in 1981, marked by an increase in violence against Jews and Jewish institutions."[14] This affects public life in the United States also. For example, in November 1982 a self-proclaimed Nazi ran as a Republican for the school board in a St. Petersburg suburb, and the party leadership of the county did not remove him from the ticket.[15]

Unfortunately, some of the recent incidents of anti-Semitism indicate that several varieties of it have become fashionable. Not only is the anti-Semitism of the bar room mirrored by that of the board room (where it has kept Jewish people out of certain clubs and jobs), it now has political voice and relevance, as reflected in the 1981 AWACS debate. Using classical anti-Semitic scapegoating tactics, a prominent U.S. Senator repeatedly told colleagues that if the AWACS sale were defeated, gas lines would appear in six months and Jews would be to blame. Similar warnings from past presidents and the present administration were used to sway votes on the decision.[16]

The November 1974 statement of General Brown, then chairman of the Joint Chiefs of Staff, may well reflect the extent of recent anti-Jewish sentiment in the United States: "They own, you know, the banks in this country, the newspapers. Just look at where the Jewish money is. . . . [The Jewish lobby is] so strong you wouldn't believe it now."[17] This illustrates one symptom of the creeping sickness unveiled by a recent Harris poll: thirty per cent of the people in the United States are anti-Semitic.[18]

The appearance of this anti-Jewish attitude may vary, but the substance remains the same. Among some it parades under the disguise of anti-Zionism, a movement launched by the Soviet Union and her Arab and Eastern European allies. It uses the same slanders and accusations with some new political twists, an old lie with a new face. Others hold on to the old slogans and names. Abba Eban expressed it best.

There is, of course, no difference whatever between anti-Semitism and the denial of Israel's statehood. Classical anti-Semitism denies the equal rights of Jews as citizens within society. Anti-Zionism denies the equal rights of the Jewish people to its lawful sovereignty within the community of nations. The common principle in the two cases is discrimination. All that has happened is that the discrimination principle has been transferred from the realm of individual right to the domain of collective identity.[19]

The role of theological or religious attitudes makes up perhaps the most distressing aspect of anti-Semitism. These attitudes find expression in a number of statements: God is through with the Jewish people; Jews are guilty of Jesus' execution; they were scattered and persecuted because they rejected Jesus; the church has taken over all of Israel's promised blessings, leaving only the biblical curses for the Jews. Sunday-school materials subtly reflect similar sentiments by picturing Old Testament characters, Jesus and the apostles as European or Anglo-Saxon rather than Jewish.

A recent survey revealed the depths of anti-Jewish feelings especially among conservative churches. The survey found that while 23% of the liberal Protestants and 32% of the Catholics were anti-Semitic, 38% of conservative Protestants were.[20] A couple of examples reinforce these findings. In 1975 at one of the nation's leading Bible schools, posters announcing a Jewish prayer group's meeting were covered over with Nazi swastikas. In 1976 a student at one of the country's foremost seminaries dogmatically asserted, "The Jews deserve everything that's been done to them, including the Holocaust." And so the malady continues.

A recent study adds:

There is abroad in our land a large measure of indifference to the most profound apprehensions of the Jewish people; a blandness and apathy in dealing with anti-Jewish behavior; a widespread incapacity or unwillingness to comprehend the necessity of the existence of Israel to Jewish safety and survival throughout the world. This is the heart of the new anti-Semitism.[21]

The Facts about the Jews

Since it is important to be able to respond to the various anti-Jewish accusations, let us look at certain facts. Is God through with the Jewish people? No, not even temporarily. Witness their supernatural preservation and modern Israel's rise in fulfillment of prophecy. Isaiah 49 provides further evidence of God's attitude toward the Jewish people. Verse 14 complains that God has set them aside. Verses 15-16 respond, "Mothers don't neglect their nursing children. Yet, even though this might occasionally happen, God says he will not act this way toward Israel. He has permanently imprinted the Jewish people on the palms of his hands, so he cannot forget them. Furthermore, Jerusalem is always in his mind's eye."

Jeremiah 31:34-36 makes an even stronger statement. God states that only under certain conditions will he reject the Jewish people for their disobedience. These conditions include the measuring of the universe, the thorough exploration of the earth's foundations and the abolition of nature's laws, e.g., the courses of the sun, moon and stars, and the cycle of the tides. Since none of these conditions has taken place, God has not set the Jewish people aside.

The New Testament reinforces this. Romans 11:1-2 asks, "Did God reject His people?" It answers with the strongest possible no available in Greek, the text's original language. Romans 3:3-4 takes the question a step further: "Didn't the Jewish people's unbelief nullify their place in God's program?" It answers with the same strong no. In fact, Romans 11:29 bluntly asserts that God's choice of the Jews cannot be revoked. Although presently God is spiritually dealing with only a remnant of Jewish people, as he has always done (11:1-6), ultimately they will all be restored to God (11:26).

"But weren't the Jews scattered and persecuted because they rejected Jesus?" Actually, the dispersion took place centuries before, when Babylon swept through Judah. Only 50,000 returned from the captivity. In fact, only ten per cent of the world Jewish population lived in Palestine in Jesus' time. Both James (1:1) and Peter (1 Pet 1:1), as well as others, testify to the dispersion as an established fact.

At the time of Christ the Dispersion of the Jews had been a *fait accompli* for several centuries. The majority of the Jewish people no longer lived in Palestine.... Therefore no one has the right to say that the Jewish people "as a whole" rejected Jesus. It is entirely possible that the Jewish people "as a whole" were not even aware of his existence.[22]

Israel's enemies did destroy Jerusalem forty years after Jesus' death, but Moses had already predicted this (Deut 28:68). He cites the specific reason for the destruction as forgetting God and disobeying his laws (Deut 28:58), not rejecting the Messiah. Jesus did predict judgment on the people of his time. But he specifically focuses on the nation's leaders in his time ("this generation," not later ones; see also Lk 9:22; 20:9-19).

The question may legitimately be asked, Did the Jews even in Israel reject Jesus? The leaders, the religious-political establishment, did refuse to accept him as Messiah, yet a great number of individuals accepted him. Throngs of Jewish people wanted to make him king (Jn 6:15) and welcomed him as the Messiah (Mt 21:9). As a result, the religious leaders hesitated to arrest him (Mt 26:5). Luke 23:27 records that crowds of Jews wept because of his execution. Thousands (Acts 2:41; 4:4) and tens of thousands (Acts 21:20) trusted him after his resurrection. This included many leaders (Acts 6:7). Further, the historian Neander reports that one million Jewish people accepted Jesus as Messiah in the first century alone.

Are the Jewish people guilty of killing Jesus? Acts 4:27 makes the clearest statement about responsibility for Jesus' death: "Indeed Herod and Pontius Pilate met together with the Gentiles and the people of Israel in this city to conspire against your holy servant Jesus, whom you anointed" (NIV; see also Jesus' statement in Mt 20:18-19). Everyone was responsible. And even when the New Testament assigns more specific responsibility, its writers never include themselves even though they are also Jews. The New Testament use of the term *Jews* must be carefully distinguished. Frequently it refers solely to the nation's leaders. In John 7:12-13 John contrasts "the Jews" to "the multitudes," all of whom were also Jews. The apostles blamed the leadership, not the Jews in general; "responsibility for the crucifixion of Jesus is never founded on membership in the people of Israel but on concurrence with the attitude of the mind of the leaders."[23] Anyone, whether Jewish or Gentile, can fit this description.

Recent archaeological digs have unearthed the area in front of Pilate's judgment hall, and archaeologists have estimated that a maximum of 150 people could fit into this area. During Passover time approximately 200,000 people lived in Jerusalem, but only 150 people out of those 200,000 composed the crowd that shouted "Crucify him."[24] And these 150 consisted of the leaders and those they could induce to join them. Luke 23:27 corroborates this, indicating that crowds followed Jesus to his death, weeping. Caught by surprise, they were totally distraught over the events. As for the 150, Jesus requested, "Father, forgive them for they don't know what they're doing" (Lk 23:24). Certainly God answered this prayer. If he did not answer Jesus' prayer, we cannot expect him to answer any of ours.

What about the allegations made by General Brown? Do Jews own the U.S. banks? Jewish people make up less than one per cent of the directors and top officers of U.S. commercial and savings banks. In fact, many Jews consider banking one of the last fortresses of discrimination against them. How about newspapers? Jewish people are the principal stockholders or owners of 3.1% of America's newspapers. And according to the American Society of Newspaper Editors, Jews compose less than 2.5% of U.S. newspaper editors.[25]

General Brown said, "We all know where the Jewish money is." Where is it? According to *Fortune* magazine,

there is no basis whatever for the suggestion that Jews monopolize U.S. business and industry.... First of all, and very definitely, they do not run banking.... Something of the same situation exists in automobiles. There are only three Jews of any prominence in the executive end of manufacturing.... The coal industry is almost entirely non-Jewish. It is doubtful whether the roster of the leading 25 companies would show a single Jew from miner to manager or on up to the board of directors.... Rubber is another non-Jewish industry.... Shipping and transportation are equally non-Jewish.

A vast continent of heavy industry and finance may therefore be staked out in which Jewish participation is incidental or nonexistent. To this may be annexed other important areas into which Jews rarely penetrated, such as light and power, and telephone and telegraph, and engineering in general, and heavy machinery and lumber and dairy products. In brief, Jews are so far from controlling the most characteristic of present-day American activities that they are hardly represented in them at all.[26]

A Harvard Business School survey done for *Fortune* magazine further substantiates this. It shows that Jews hold less than one per cent of the five hundred top U.S. corporation positions. The situation is such that in many places "WASPs tend to get more prestigious jobs than Jews of the same educational background."[27]

General Brown also referred to the Jewish people's political influence. Through two hundred years of American history a total of only 108 governors, senators or congressmen have been Jewish, and no presidents or vice presidents. By way of comparison half of the nation's first forty presidents have been Presbyterian or Episcopalian. Jews outnumber either of these denominations.[28] Jewish political power then fades as a myth. America has traditionally supported Israel not because of supposed Jewish political power but because of the public's natural inclination to support the underdog, to support a people trying to maintain their freedom, democratic way of life and security against violent opposition. Likewise many Americans believe there is a "chosenness" about Jews that should not be tampered with or challenged. They take seriously what God says about blessing and cursing (Gen 12:3), as well as his unconditional promise of the land.

In light of increasing anti-Semitism, what responsibility does the committed Christian have? First, get the facts, such as those above, and know them. God is a God of truth, and his people should reflect his character. So stand for truth. Stand up for the Jewish people and do not allow anti-Semitic statements to be made without correcting them. Join with Jewish organizations, such as the Anti-Defamation League and the American Jewish Committee, in their fight against anti-Semitism. Ask them how you can help. Write letters to newspapers or magazines if you see anti-Semitism in their pages. Finally, show love; demonstrate it in your behavior toward your Jewish acquaintances, and express your concern and shame for anti-Semitism past and present.

5
THE JEWISH PEOPLE AND THE LAND

Arguments for and against the State of Israel have raged for decades, even going back before the inception of the modern state in 1948. Christians have been found on both sides of this issue. Regardless of a person's stand on Israel, it is important to realize that the great majority of Jewish people are strongly pro-Israel and many of them perceive a Christian's response toward Israel as an indicator of his true attitude toward Jews. Therefore, it is important to be knowledgeable about the circumstances surrounding Israel and the Jewish people's concerns about the nation.

Jewish people have always been concerned about the land of Israel. Every Passover Jews express their desire to return to Jerusalem, as they have done for hundreds of years. The great Jewish sage, HaLevi, expressed it best:

Oh, city of the world, with sacred splendor blest,
My spirit yearns to thee from out the far-off West;
A stream of love wells forth when I recall thy day,

Now is thy temple waste, thy glory passed away.
Had I an eagle's wings, straight would I fly to thee,
Moisten thy holy dust with wet cheeks streaming free.
Oh, how I long for thee! Albeit thy king has gone,
Albeit where balm once flowed, the serpent dwells alone.
Could I but kiss thy dust, so would I fain expire,
As sweet as honey then, my passion, my desire.[1]

HaLevi turned the last two lines into prophecy when he returned to Israel. There, while he was praying at the Wailing Wall, an Arab horseman ran him down and killed him.

An appreciation of this feeling for the land is vital for an adequate understanding of the Jewish people.

The Right to the Land
But whose land is it? The Arabs' or the Jews'? To help answer this question we need to look at the situation in Palestine before 1948, when Israel became a state again. There had always been a Jewish presence in the land, but it began to grow significantly under the British Mandate (1917-48). The Jewish people began acquiring more land, not by threat or force, but with the help of the Arabs. Despite restrictions, landlords and peasants eagerly unloaded waste marshland and arid, uncultivated areas, usually at a high price. Actually, Jewish population growth and expansion caused no shrinkage of Arab cultivated land nor the displacement or impoverishment of Arab farmers. The acquired land had not previously been used.[2] This cooperative Arab attitude reached the highest levels. As the Arab leader Faisal I put it,

We Arabs, especially the educated among us, look with the deepest sympathy on the Zionist movement. Our deputation here in Paris is fully acquainted with the proposals submitted yesterday by the Zionist Organization to the Peace Conference, and we regard them as moderate and proper. We will do our best, insofar as we are concerned, to help them through; we will wish the Jews a most hearty welcome home.[3]

It is unfortunate that this attitude did not linger.

A look at the distribution of the land ownership of Palestine in 1948 is enlightening. Jewish people owned 8.6% of the land. Israeli Arabs owned 3.3%. Arab owners abandoned another 16.9%. By law this reverts to the government in control, Great Britain. In 1917 Britain received a mandate from the League of Nations to govern Palestine. As mandatory power, Great Britain owned 71.2% of the land, passed on to Britain from Turkey, the previous owner. By international law, at the re-establishment of the State of Israel, Great Britain passed this land on to the Israeli government. Therefore, Jews owned 96.7% of the land by right of purchase, possession or decree of international law.[4]

Beyond the situation existing at the time of Israel's re-establishment, several other bases exist for the Jewish people's right to the land of Israel. In the Bible God promised the land to Abraham and his descendants (Gen 12:7). Here he specifies the land then known as Canaan. God later repeats and expands the promises concerning the land (Gen 13:14-18). At this time (v. 15) he explicitly states he is promising the land *forever;* he makes an eternal promise. He confirms this promise to Isaac (Gen 17:19) and then to Jacob and his descendants (Gen 28:12-13). Other Scripture passages reinforce and repeat these promises (Gen 15:18-21; 17:6-8; Ex 23:31; Num 34:1-5; Deut 7:1-8; Jer 31:31-40; 33:6-18; and more). Unquestionably, God promised the land to the Jewish people forever.

Have these promises been revoked? An investigation of the New Testament indicates a definite no. Stephen in his defense speech (Acts 7:1-8) refers to God's covenant with Abraham in a way which assumes its continuing character (v. 5), and he says nothing about its being altered in any way. In a major New Testament teaching (Gal 3:8-18), several things stand out. Since men do not annul or alter covenants they make (vv. 15, 17), no one can change a covenant confirmed by God himself. This covenant includes the inheritance, including the land promised to Abraham. It is based on God's promise and so is unconditional, dependent on God and not man. Verse 14, speaking of Gentile participation in these blessings, would have been the ideal place to say that God no longer intended the covenant promises for Israel but for the church. Paul does not say this. Therefore, the covenant remains intact for Israel. Jesus came to confirm, not set aside, the covenants and promises (Rom 15:8; Mt 5:17).

Hebrews 6:13-19 reinforces this perspective. Two unshakable, unchangeable things form the foundation for God's covenant with

Abraham—his oath and his promise. This makes the covenant itself unchangeable and its fulfillment certain. Romans 9:4 adds that the covenants and promises still belong to the Jewish people. So the passage clearly affirms their continuing validity. Further, Israel's unbelief does not affect their fulfillment; God will see to it that they will be carried out (Rom 3:3-4; 11:1-2). Romans 11:29 sums it all up by saying God's gifts "are irrevocable." Therefore, God gave the covenants and promises, including the land of Israel, to the Jewish people forever.

In addition to the biblical evidence, the Jews' claim to the land has other support. Historical and archaeological evidence shows that the Canaanites lived in the land prior to Abraham but have long since disappeared. The Jewish people succeeded the Canaanites and have ever since maintained a continuous presence in the land.

James Parkes, a noted historian, has shown that as many Jews as possible have always lived in the land. Two factors have determined their population in the land: how many the land would economically support and how many the political authorities would allow.[5] Artifacts and ruins uncovered by archaeologists confirm this continuous Jewish presence from earliest times and show no Arab presence until the seventh century A.D. The Arabs controlled Palestine only in the period between 637 and 1071. Thereafter the Turks, who are not Arabs, controlled the area. Despite the Turkish government's policy severely restricting Jewish immigration, the Jewish people maintained a continuous presence in Palestine under Turkish control. Moreover, in many cases the Arabs were the immigrants, not the Jews. The influx of Arab people into the area came during the British Mandate as a result of good wages and higher standards of living. For example, British census figures show that between 1922 and 1939 the Arab population of Haifa increased 200%.

International law substantiates the Jewish claim as well. Great Britain replaced Turkey as the internationally recognized and constituted authority over Palestine during World War I. She confirmed the Balfour Declaration, originally made in 1917, which states: "His Majesty's Government views with favor the establishment in Palestine of a national home for the Jewish people, and will use their best endeavors to facilitate the achievement of this object."

The 1947 United Nations resolution establishing Israel as the Jewish state conferred international recognition and legitimacy on Israel. It divided Palestine between the Arabs and Jews and established two states: a Palestinian Arab state and a Jewish state.

The Jewish people also have the right to the land by purchase and possession. Jews had purchased segments of the land prior to the nation's establishment. After the UN resolution Jewish people settled the land, much of which had been abandoned and unused. In accord with due process of law, the land controlled by the mandatory power passed on to the newly established state. Therefore, as previously noted, Jewish Israelis officially owned 96.7% of the land. Apart from a few exceptions, Jews did not confiscate the land; they purchased it and made reparations wherever possible. By and large, Arabs who did not leave Israel or fight against her have maintained their property rights. And Israel even invited back those Arabs who left in 1948.

In addition, the land belongs to the Jewish people by the right of cultivation and use. Simply put, the Arabs had left the land barren and uncultivated. The Israelis cultivated the land and made it productive, investing much labor and capital. This further establishes their claim.

The last area of evidence to support the Jewish claim to Israel, the right to the land by military conquest, may be somewhat disagreeable. Throughout the many years of Middle East wars, the Arabs have consistently attacked Israel. Nevertheless, the Israelis have won on the battlefield mainly the land granted to them by international law. It is internationally recognized that the winner in a war is not forced to return land it has won. In the 1948 war, for example, Jordan captured the internationalized city of Jerusalem and was not required to return it to international control.

Further, if the present occupants returned all land to its original owners, many nations would have to return land and large numbers of people would have to move. America would then be restored to the Indians, and we would have to return to the lands of our ancestors. Even if this occurred, the Jewish people would retain their right to the land. They remain the closest thing to the original owners of Israel, initially with borders much larger than they now have. The Jews have always been eager to live at peace with their Arab neighbors. They accepted the partitioned state in 1948. The Arabs rejected it and resorted to warfare, but failed to establish their claim in this way as well.

An evaluation of the evidence substantiates the conclusion that the land rightfully belongs to the Jews. But what do the Arabs have to look forward to? Isaiah 19:19-24 pictures a future when the Arabs and Israelis will live together in harmony, and God will bless the Arabs as well as the Jewish people. God does have a purpose for the Arabs, but not at the expense of the Jewish people.

The Relevant Issues

In the rest of this chapter, we will explore several relevant issues. But first I want to make clear that affirming the Jewish right to the land does not imply condoning all the Israeli government does. Most U.S. citizens stand solidly behind our nation; yet few would agree with all the federal government does. In the same way, we can stand solidly behind Israel without agreeing with everything her leaders do. Supporting Israel also does not imply hating the Arabs. We are responsible to love them while still maintaining our firm support of Israel.

A study of U.S. support for Israel reveals some surprising facts. The eleven Arab nations participating in the Yom Kippur War received 8.9 billion dollars in assistance from the U.S. government and American oil companies during the six years before the war. During this same time the Soviet Union gave more than 3.7 billion dollars to the Arabs. On the other hand, over the same period, the U.S. gave Israel only 2 billion dollars.[6] U.S. support of Israel is certainly not lopsided, as some critics claim. Add to this a comparison of the Arab states with Israel: 20 nations to 1; 130 million people to 3 million; infinitely greater financial resources from oil; at least a 4-1 advantage in all phases of military equipment and personnel. This brings up the question, Who is in greater need of aid? Or for that matter, Who has always been our staunchest and most valuable (and often, only) ally in the Middle East, and its only democratic nation?

Writers have spilled a lot of ink discussing refugee problems. The problem of the Palestinian refugees definitely exists, but they have already received far more international aid than any other group in history. Israel should take a hand in solving these problems but is not morally responsible for them. She cannot be morally expected to give up her legitimate national rights to solve them. To balance the picture, we should be aware that 800,000 Jewish refugees from Arab countries now live in Israel. They have eight to ten billion dollars in reparation claims for goods and property they were forced to leave behind.[7] These people lost their homes, lands, goods and money in Arab lands. No Arab government made any attempt to make reparations. Israel simply absorbed these people and assisted their entrance into Israeli society. By contrast, the UN Economic Survey Commission found a maximum of 726,000 Arab refugees from Israel, over 100,000 of whom have returned to their homes.[8] This raises a legitimate question, Who has had the real refugee problem?

Many people have pointed to the Palestinian problem as the major cause of Middle Eastern unrest. But here again, a broader perspective produces a more adequate understanding. The idea of a Palestinian nationality is quite recent. Until British rule over Palestine, the countryside consisted mainly of small towns. These small towns, or specific sections of land they lived and worked on, and not Palestine, held the people's loyalties. In fact, until the twentieth century most Middle Eastern national aspirations focused on identification with Syria.

Moreover, never in history has Palestine ever been a nation, let alone an Arab nation.[9] The name originates from the biblical term used for the land of Philistines. In A.D. 135, long after the Philistines had ceased to exist as a people, the Romans brought the term back, as the name for Israel and Judah, as part of an attempt to wipe out any traces of Jewish identity and nationhood. Five hundred years later, after the Arabs conquered the area, they treated Palestine (or Filastin) as part of Syria. While they attributed national identity and character to other areas such as Egypt, Iraq, Arabia and Yemen, they never so identified Palestine. After the coming of the Crusaders, and also with the Moslem reconquest in the eleventh century, the term *Filastin* disappeared even as part of Syria. This continued under the Ottoman Empire (1516-1917), which designated the area Southern Syria.

Throughout this whole period (135-1917) the inhabitants—except for the Jews allowed to remain there—never had a distinctive national identity, and the land was characterized by intertribal warfare. In fact, in the nineteenth century, masses of Egyptians and Syrians moved in and through the area, further adding to the mix of peoples there.

After World War I the European powers broke up the Ottoman Empire and distributed its lands. At this time two groups laid claim to these territories, the Arab nation and the Jewish people. Both were recognized as legitimate by international law, with neither claim being viewed as an encroachment on the other (see Faisal I's statement on p. 52). Eventually Arab states were created to fulfill the Arab claim. The Jewish claim was to be satisfied with the newly named area of Palestine, which at that time included what is now Israel, the West Bank and Jordan. The establishment of the League of Nations in 1919 validated in law this distribution of lands. The division was such that the allocation for the Arabs was more than a hundred times greater in area and countless times richer in resources than was the Palestine of the Jews.

Then in 1922, to appease an important Bedouin leader, eighty per cent of the Jewish land was cut away to establish the kingdom of Jordan—which had had no historical existence before this time —and provide land for Arabs in Palestine. During the British Mandate (1917-48) 300,000 Arabs migrated to Palestine, attracted by the high standard of living created by the Jewish people rebuilding their ancient home. So Palestine was truly Jewish and not Arab. In fact, before 1948 the term *Palestinian* referred to a Jewish person living in Palestine. For example, the Jewish brigade in the British army in World War II wore *Palestine* on their shoulders.

Further, the Palestinian issue does not revolve around the problem of a people expelled from their land. Most Palestinians (eighty per cent) still live within the territory formerly called Palestine.[10] In 1948 Arab leaders told Israeli Arabs to evacuate Israel, while the Jewish leaders urged them to stay.[11] The Arabs who left Israel, left by choice; they were not forced out. Neither is the Palestinian issue a problem mainly of refugees. Of the 2.8 million Palestinian Arabs, only 600,000 live as refugees in the refugee camps.[12] These refugees remain in the camps in Arab nations while many Arab countries suffer manpower shortages. As a result experts on refugee problems have called for their resettlement in these countries as the only practical solution. Arab governments have apparently gone to extremes to keep this from occurring. The Kuwaiti newspaper *Al-Qabas* (Sept 24, 1974) reported that the Arab League had asked the Kuwaiti government not to grant citizenship to Palestinians living in Kuwait. Among the Arab League countries only Jordan has permitted Palestinians to gain citizenship. Abdul Razak Kader, the Algerian political writer now living in exile, perceptively noted:

The nationalists of the states neighboring on Israel, whether they are in the government or in business, whether Palestinian, Syrian, or Lebanese, or town dweller or of tribal origin, all know that at the beginning of the century and during the British Mandate the marshy plains and stony hills were sold to the Zionists by their fathers or uncles for gold, the very gold which is often the origin of their own political or commercial careers. The nomadic or semi-nomadic peasants who inhabited the frontier regions know full well what the green plains, the afforested hills and the flowering fields of today's Israel were like before.

The Palestinians who are today refugees in the neighboring countries and who were adults at the time of their flight know all this, and no anti-Zionist propaganda—pan-Arab or pan-Moslem—can make them forget that their present nationalist exploiters are the worthy sons of their feudal exploiters of yesterday and that the thorns of their life are of Arab, not Jewish origin.[13]

Historically, resettlement, not repatriation, has best solved refugee problems, but the Arab governments have continually refused to acknowledge this. They have simply not tried to solve the problem of homelessness, as the Israelis did with the refugees coming to Israel. The Arabs have put the refugees in retention camps rather than using some of their oil income and their open lands to help resettle them. In fact, the Arab nations have repeatedly thwarted attempts to resettle the Palestinians. As the late G. Douglas Young, former head of the American Institute of Holy Land Studies, noted:

70,000 [refugees] were accepted back into Israel under a reunification of families program after the 1948-49 war. Israel offered in

August 1949 to take back another 100,000. The offer was rejected by the Arab states. Israel released ten million dollars of blocked bank balances held by Arab refugees without any conditions or *quid pro quo*. All UNRWA proposals for refugee settlement were rejected or blocked by the Arab states. The proposal of Eric Johnston, special envoy of President Eisenhower, for the irrigation of the Jordan Valley to allow resettlement of 240,000 refugees was also rejected by the Arab League in October 1955.[14] The Palestinian issue does not really involve a problem of a citizenless people. Most Palestinian Arabs (67%) have citizenship in the countries they reside in. The problem is also not the lack of a Palestinian state. Jordan fills that role. In fact, it remains the only Palestinian Arab state in all history. Most Palestinians are Jordanians, and most Jordanians are Palestinians.[15] The Israelis accepted the UN partition into the Jewish and Palestinian states, but many Palestinians and all neighboring Arab countries did not and so began a war against Israel. From the beginning, Israel has not opposed a just settlement to the Palestinian question. The Arabs have hindered the progress.

Although this is not well known, Israel and the U.S. maintain extensive regular contacts with Palestinians, and Israel encourages full and open economic relations with those of the West Bank, Gaza and Jordan. Israel has consistently maintained that she will not enter into an overall Middle Eastern settlement that doesn't solve the Palestinian problem. Contrast this with the attitude of the Arabs, as revealed by Zuhair Muhsin, head of the PLO military operations department, in an interview with a Dutch paper:

> There are no differences between Jordanians, Palestinians, Syrians and Lebanese.... We are all one people.... It is of national interest for the Arabs to encourage the existence of the Palestinians against Zionism [the PLO codeword for the nation Israel and Jewish presence in the land]. Yes, the existence of a separate Palestinian identity is there only for tactical reasons. The establishment of a Palestinian state is a new expedient to continue the fight against Zionism and for Arab unity.[16]

A New Arab State?
PLO and Arab spokesmen have proposed the establishment of a

secular, democratic state in the area as a solution of the problem. However, no Arab state today is secular and democratic. All are Muslim, and none are democratic. In nearly all, minorities face grim situations. For example, the number of Christians in Arab countries has declined steadily as a result of pressures on them.[17] The Arab states also have a long record of oppressing Jewish minorities. In an interview in the Chicago Daily News, a Jewish woman who escaped from Syria described her life: "After primary school, there was no high school for us, and no chance to work in an office or bank. We were forbidden this kind of work. We were surrounded by hatred. Sometimes there were attacks on us when we went to synagogue."[18]

In the Manchester Guardian a refugee from Iraq described the treatment of the Jewish people there as including "discrimination, persecution and pogroms since 1933 when Iraq became independent." In both these countries arrest, torture and excessive restrictions on communication, movement and business operations remain a regular part of life for Jews.[19] Before 1948, even the treatment in Palestine did not differ. David Landes, Harvard history professor, reported:

> The Jews of Palestine were designated as inferior (in law as well as custom), segregated by appearance and residence, subject to discrimination and abuse, and liable to sporadic and not infrequent violence. Lynching... was not a common occurrence; but it happened often enough, and then with impunity, to constitute an immanent, imminent menace.[20]

Should Jewish people expect it to be any different if a secular, democratic state replaces Israel? A secure Israel remains the only place in the world where Jewish people can be free from oppression, persecution and anti-Semitism and be freely Jewish.

For that matter, can a unified state where Jews and Muslims live together really exist? The Palestinians recently destroyed a Lebanon where Christians and Muslims had lived in peace for years. This shows that a PLO dominated mini-state on the West Bank would endanger Jews and Christians alike, and eventually even Jordanians, as it did the Lebanese. Lebanese Christians learned, as did the Kurds in Iraq earlier, that Arab states have little room for tolerating separate minorities.

Would the establishment of a Palestinian state between Israel and Jordan solve the conflict? Camille Chamoun, Lebanese Interior Minister, asserted: "I have served the Palestinian cause for thirty-five years, and I never thought the day would come when I would regret it. . . . I don't know how they [the Palestinians] can ask for a country of their own after all the crimes they committed in Lebanon.[21]

Further, a definite threat exists that the Arabs and Russians would arm this new state to the teeth. Given the Palestinians' commitments, this could easily insure Israel's destruction. During an interview with NBC on January 12, 1976, reporters confronted PLO representative Shafik al-Hout. "Recently there have been some reports out of the Mideast that the PLO would settle for the West Bank and Gaza Strip and allow Israel to exist as a country." Asked if this was true, he replied, "No." Al-Hout later added, "If you mean a pure Jewish state, there will be no Jewish state."[22] On March 30, 1976, PLO leader Arafat stood beside George Habash, the leader of the radical terrorist group responsible for hijacking a French airliner to Entebbe, Uganda. Arafat said: "We will continue our struggle in spirit and blood until we succeed in establishing our secular democratic state over the entire territory of Palestine. There is no difference between myself and Dr. Habash.[23]

PLO documents (available without charge from the Consulate General of Israel) plainly spell out their commitments: the control of all Palestine and Israel's destruction. The ten-point political program of the PLO (1974) states:

> The PLO will struggle by all means, foremost of which is armed struggle, to liberate Palestinian land and to establish the people's national, independent and fighting authority on every part of Palestinian land to be liberated.

> The PLO will struggle against any plan for the establishment of a Palestinian entity, the price of which is recognition of Israel, conciliation, secure borders.

The Palestinian National Charter (1968) asserts in Article 9: "Armed struggle is the only way to liberate Palestine. Thus it is the overall strategy, not merely a tactical phase. The Palestinian Arab people assert their absolute determination and firm resolution to continue their armed struggle."

Never retracted, these statements have been repeated by, among others, Yasir Arafat:

This war has just started. We are just beginning to get ready for what will be a long, long war; a war that will run for generations. ... The goal of our struggle is the end of Israel, and there can be no compromises or mediations. ... We don't want peace, we want victory. Peace for us means Israel's destruction and nothing else.[24]

In a recent interview Farouk Kaddoumi, the PLO Foreign Minister and a moderate, said, "I shall make it perfectly clear to you. We shall never recognize Israel." The interviewer responded, "Your attitude means the destruction of Israel." Said Kaddoumi, "Yes, I want to destroy the enemy."[25]

More unfortunate is the attitude of the so-called moderate nations of the Middle East. Saudi Arabia is the most prominent of these countries. Yet, as cited in the Saudi daily paper, then Saudi Crown Prince—now King—Fahd has stated, "There is no doubt that the day will come when Israel will finally be liquidated. ... The day will come when Israel will be paralyzed and nobody will be able to help it, not even by giving it nuclear weapons."[26] In view of the PLO's stated purposes and even the "moderate" Arabs' supportive attitudes, it would be unwise to establish a Palestinian state between Israel and Jordan. This would merely give more tangible opportunity to further Israel's ultimate destruction.

Recent Problems

Recently world attention has focused on two more issues. The first deals with Jewish control over Jerusalem. The recent discussion has neglected several facts. All four quarters of Jerusalem were very Jewish until British rule and have been inhabited by the Jewish people for the last few centuries.[27] Palestinian Jews have made up a majority of Jerusalem's population since 1840. Further, the city has served as the capital of only one nation in history, Israel.[28] The 1947 UN resolution established Jerusalem as an internationalized city accessible to all religious groups. In 1948 Jordan seized the city and controlled it until 1967. During this time Jordan restricted Jewish access to the city and set out to obliterate the city's Jewish past. Jordanian officials destroyed the Jewish quarter, demolished or desecrated 58 synagogues and turned those that were not destroyed into toilets, stables and chicken coops. They also used Jewish slabs from the Mount of Olives graveyard to pave the walks of Jordanian generals' homes. Earlier, even the British had prohibited Jews from visiting the gravesites of Abraham, Isaac and Jacob. Only under Israeli rule have all faiths had free access to Jerusalem. As the Pope's Apostolic Representative put it, "Christians never had it so good as under this government."[29]

The other issue involves the disturbances on the West Bank, formerly part of Jordan. In an interview, Farah el-Araj, a West Bank mayor, helped put the unrest in perspective. He called the unrest relatively minor when compared to the riots against the Jordanian government in the 1960s. "Frankly, it is occupation here, ... but it's more similar to the British mandate than to Jordan's rule. We are much freer as a municipality now than under Jordanian rule."[30]

The equation of Zionism with racism deserves some attention. Zionism represents the Jewish people's national liberation movement, their response to the problems of oppression, persecution, anti-Semitism and extermination. Zionism seeks to establish a peaceful Jewish national homeland where Jews from all over the world can come and be freely, safely Jewish. Is this racism? The recognized "father of Zionism," Theodore Herzl, said: "Once I have witnessed the redemption of Israel, my people, I wish to assist in the redemption of the Africans."[31] This certainly doesn't represent a racist sentiment. Faisal I, an early Arab leader, concurs with this assessment.

With the chiefs of your movement [the Zionist movement], especially with Dr. Weizmann, we have had and continue to have the closest relations. He has been a great helper to our cause, and I hope the Arabs may soon be in a position to make the Jews some return for their kindness. We are working together for a reformed and revived Near East, and our two movements complete one another. The Jewish movement is national and not imperialist. Our movement is national and not imperialist, and there is room for us both. Indeed, I think that neither can be a real success without the other.[32]

The various races of people living in Israel further demonstrate

Zionism's nonracist character. Africans, Asians, Europeans, North and South Americans all contribute to Israel's Jewish population, truly a multiracial group. The election of Toufik Zayad, an Arab Communist, as mayor of Nazareth provides still more evidence for Israel's nonracist character. A racist state would never allow this. For example, a Syrian Jew could never be elected mayor of Damascus.

Who are the real racists?

Eldridge Cleaver testifies:

Having lived intimately for several years among the Arabs, I know them to be among the most racist people on earth. This is particularly true of their attitude toward Black people. . . . Many Arab families that can afford to, keep one or two Black slaves to do their menial labor. Sometimes they own an entire family. I have seen such slaves with my own eyes.[33]

In words echoing Hitler's *Mein Kampf* and the long-discredited *Protocols of the Elders of Zion*, Jordan's ambassador to the United Nations, Hazem Nuseibeh, during a General Assembly debate on December 8, 1980, described the Jewish conspiracy which "controls, manipulates and exploits the rest of humanity by controlling the money and wealth of the world." He concluded, "It is a well-known fact that the Zionists are the richest people in the world and control much of its destiny," thus completely ignoring the ironic fact that his statement accurately describes not the Jews, but his own Arab people and the results of petrodollars and oil diplomacy.

While his statements stunned the United Nations, they were by no means unrepresentative of the official Jordanian attitude to Jewish people. Jordan, a "moderate" Arab nation, may well be the only nation whose law expressly forbids Jewish people from being citizens (Civil Law No. 6, paragraph 3).

Consistent in its policy of discrimination against Jews, Jordan has banned appearances by outstanding Jewish performers such as Danny Kaye and Isaac Stern. It has also prohibited performances showing Jews in a favorable light. In fact, on September 22, 1978, Radio Amman went so far as to call for a holy war against Jews.[34]

Now, who are the real racists?

The PLO Campaign against Israel

Several premises have regularly distorted most people's percep-
tions of the Middle East situation. The Israeli attempt to clear the
PLO military forces out of Lebanon during the summer of 1982
brought two of them to the surface: that Israel should be judged
differently from other countries, and that the PLO is a moderate
liberation movement. Instead of rushing to condemn Israel, as
many with little or no sense of history and geography have done,
we should heed the words of Senator Bob Packwood of Oregon.
In a June 1980 speech still relevant today, he reminded his colleagues:

Review this history once more: time after time, war after war,
decade after decade, terrorism and fighting within the bounds
of the State of Israel; time after time Israel taking territory and
giving it back, taking it and giving it back, hoping for peace and
getting more war. . . .

What do you think this country would do if we had bands of
terrorists getting in their rubber boats in Baja, California, and
rowing up north of San Diego and shooting bazookas at buses
full of schoolchildren? What do you think this country would
do if we had terrorists rowing across any of the Great Lakes into
our country and killing and maiming children, women and
others? This country would be so incensed that we would chase
those terrorists back into their lairs, bomb them and their territory, and probably seize it, and feel we had an absolute right to
do so.

Israel does the same thing, and consistently resolutions are
passed by the United Nations condemning them for doing the
same thing that any other country would think it had a right
to do.[35]

While the media recounted the battle in Lebanon in graphic detail,
they neglected to report what preceded it. No one mentioned the
situation in northern Israel, where children had to ride their school
buses with a daily armed guard, where families spent countless
nights—and days—in bomb shelters, due to regular PLO attacks
and shelling from southern Lebanon. They also forgot to headline
the kibbutz nursery where the PLO held three-year-old children
hostage and killed one before the others were rescued. This was

just the beginning, as far as the PLO was concerned. Captured PLO documents include orders for the shelling, occupation and destruction of five northern Israeli towns, scheduled for July 28-29, 1982, just weeks after the Israelis moved on the terrorist strongholds. Not only did the Israeli army discover the PLO actively arming and preparing for hostilities—and this in blatant violation of the cease-fire they had agreed to—they found the Syrian army in Lebanon at an advanced stage of preparation for an attack on Israel as well.

The eyewitness accounts, the captured documents and the sheer immensity of the arms stockpiled in PLO enclaves all verify the transformation of the PLO from a terrorist gang into a full-fledged terrorist army intent on liquidating Israel. Weapons and ammunition of every shape and size—including some that were outlawed by international treaties—were discovered. For over a week ten truckloads of arms a day were carried from one storage space alone. Four hundred truckloads of weapons were carted from another hideout just a few miles from the Israeli border. The Israeli forces found weapons from all over the world: the Soviet Union, China, Vietnam, North Korea, Eastern Europe, Libya, and even from the United States. Some of the U.S. weapons still had their original shipping cartons showing they had been sold to Saudi Arabia— and thus transferred to the PLO in direct violation of Saudi agreements with the United States. The crates containing the arms were frequently marked "tractor parts" or stamped with the Red Crescent, the Islamic Red Cross. Arms were found everywhere: in mosques, schools, homes, hospitals, public buildings and even at UN offices. Along with the weapons were copies of Hitler's Mein Kampf in Arabic, and in one location, a written agreement between the UN peacekeeping forces and the PLO actually allowing the placement of a gun nest for shelling northern Israel. All told, the captured arsenal could supply an army of over 100,000 men. Apparently the PLO had the excess weapons ready for other forces who would join them in a sneak attack on Israel.

The captured documents show the company the PLO keeps. Its fighters were trained in the Soviet Union, China, Cuba, Eastern Europe and other Soviet satellites. Some of these countries, and Libya as well, even provided personnel for the PLO army. The PLO, in turn, trained, armed and advised terrorist organizations which read like an international "most wanted" list: the Red Brigades (who kidnaped U.S. General Dozier in Italy), the Japanese Red Army, the Baadar-Meinhoff Gang, the IRA, the Iranian Mujaheddin (who coordinated the takeover of the U.S. embassy in Iran), as well as the terrorists in El Salvador and Nicaragua. These, then, are the associates of a terrorist organization bent on permanent war against the Jewish people and those who sympathize with them.

Their tactics in battle expose more of the PLO's basic commitments and morality. They placed heavy artillery pieces in hospitals and located headquarters and main positions in schools and heavily populated areas, as did the Syrian forces in Lebanon. PLO fighters fought from inside schools, hospitals and mosques. Knowing that Israeli soldiers don't shoot children, they sent twelve-year-old boys with rocket-propelled grenades against Israeli troops. In many cases PLO soldiers hid behind rows of women and children while firing on Israeli forces. They also refused to share their food with Lebanese civilians and, in fact, blocked the distribution of UN-supplied food to refugees in Beirut. Moreover, as Franklin Graham (son of Billy Graham) wrote of his own experience in Beirut: "On Sunday [August 1] as the PLO counterattacked, they pointed guns not to the advancing Israeli Army, but to civilian areas all over East Beirut, where Sami and many of his church members live. Many rockets and artillery shells landed in the villages near Sami's home. Innocent civilians died that day at the hands of the PLO, and western reporters ignored it."[36] Other eyewitness reports indicated that retreating PLO forces frequently slaughtered people in their homes to raise the death toll blamed on the Israeli army.

The PLO's stay in Lebanon was as brutal as its exit. Before the Israeli attack, from the start of the 1975-76 Civil War initiated by the PLO and its allies and the subsequent arrival of the Syrian "peacekeeping forces," nearly 100,000 people were killed in Lebanon, according to the American Lebanese League. The PLO massacred Lebanese citizens, destroyed their homes and took over their farms and cities. They stole cars, robbed vineyards and ruined orchards. Girls were molested, and so schools were shut down for the safety of the children. The extent of this horror came out as the Lebanese started talking to the reporters following the Israeli army. No wonder the people of Lebanon welcomed the Israeli forces with flowers, cheers and celebrations, as well as with slogans such as "Death to Arafat. Long live Begin." The Israelis were their liberators from years of devastation. This Lebanese response correlates with the extreme reluctance of other Arab nations to open their doors to the PLO leaving Lebanon. After all, these were their Arab brothers whose cause they had championed. But they also knew them for the terrorists and murderers they really are. These nations saw what the PLO did to Lebanon and almost did to Jordan before King Hussein drove them out, and they did not want any part of them.

Agreements Violated by the PLO

The PLO's record in keeping agreements is equally lamentable, as the situation in Lebanon again illustrates. Since 1969, the PLO has signed three major agreements and two secondary ones restricting its role in Lebanon. In them the PLO promised to respect Lebanon's sovereignty and refrain from terrorism against Israel launched from Lebanese territory. It has blatantly violated all five agreements made to, through and by Arab brothers, precipitated civil war in Lebanon, and in the process helped destroy the government and nation of Lebanon.

After Israel responded to vicious shellings of its northern towns in 1981, the United States helped arrange a cease-fire. The PLO promptly flouted it by its massive military build-up along Israel's borders, in direct violation of the terms they had agreed to. During the negotiations for an agreement in Lebanon in 1982, the PLO systematically engaged in "controlled" violations of the interim cease-fire in order to inflict casualties on Israel and provoke sufficient retaliation to have Israel blamed for upsetting the negotiations. The media repeatedly swallowed the bait. At the same time, while publicly mouthing its desire to leave, the PLO fortified its positions and dug in even further.

After an agreement was finally reached despite the PLO's repeatedly putting forward preconditions which almost sabotaged it from the start, the PLO persisted in its duplicity. The agreed-upon evacuation plan required the terrorists to turn over their arms to the Lebanese army. Instead, as Lebanese, U.S. and Israeli officials all noted, the PLO gave its heavy weapons and extensive ammunition stores to its allies, the leftist militias. In order not to undermine the agreement, the Begin government allowed the withdrawal to proceed despite this direct violation. Further violating the agreement, the PLO did not register all its fighters and instead included women and children in the number of those leaving Beirut in order to confuse the count of the terrorists withdrawing.

When they entered West Beirut after the leftist assassination of President-elect Bashir Gemayel and a score of his associates, the Israeli forces had to locate two thousand PLO soldiers hiding there in still another violation of the evacuation agreement. In one building alone, as CBS reported, they discovered twenty-four tons of weapons and ammunition, another violation. Ultimately, the Lebanese army discovered a four-mile maze of tunnels interconnecting several key Palestinian refugee camps. An underground city, the tunnels contained shelters and food storage rooms as well as stacks of arms and ammunition, stolen vehicles, helicopters and even a small submarine. All this was to have been turned over to the Lebanese army. This demonstrates once again the PLO's callous disregard for agreements it makes.

The actions of the Israeli forces stand in stark contrast to this. The army followed the Jewish policy of *Tohar Haneshek* ("humane fighting"). According to eyewitnesses, Israeli soldiers distributed their rations to needy Lebanese, gave out blankets and restored water and electricity to villages, and made concerted efforts to spare the lives and property of civilians, frequently at the cost of their own lives. At Tyre and Sidon, before the fighting began, Israeli planes dropped leaflets and used loudspeakers to warn the people to leave the cities in order not to get hurt. In Tyre, the army waited an extra two hours—and risked getting stuck in the dark— at the request of the Red Cross representative. Individual acts stand out as well. In one village, while under attack, Israeli soldiers took a mother in labor to a hospital. On another occasion an entire armored column stopped while under fire to save the life of a lost, wounded baby. These are just a few examples of the code of behavior followed by the Israeli forces, but they never made the papers.

One-Sided Press Coverage

In fact, the press coverage was badly distorted. After a personal inspection of Lebanon, Rep. Charles Wilson of Texas said at a July 2, 1982, press conference that the press coverage of Lebanon "has been unfair.... The reporting has been very one-sided." Rep. Mark Siljander of Michigan later added his personal observations. Although the press had not reported it, he related, "the people expressed feelings of relief and appreciation to the Israelis" for relieving them from the burden and oppression of the PLO. He also pointed out that the media's reporting of casualties and damage caused by the Israeli operation "were grossly exaggerated."

For example, originally Red Cross organizations—one of which is headed by Yasir Arafat's brother Fathi—reported that there were 600,000 refugees made homeless in southern Lebanon, which is more than the total population of southern Lebanon. The figures have since declined; the latest was 20,000 and still dropping. The media first reported 10,000 killed in Tyre and Sidon. The Bishop of Tyre, however, revealed there were only fifty people killed there, while local authorities in Sidon listed 100 fatalities as the official figure for their municipality.

The rubble photographed as Israeli tanks rolled through Tyre, Sidon, Damour and Beirut showed great devastation. But no one mentioned in their dispatches that this wasteland was the result of the 1975-76 Civil War and not due to the Israeli operations. For example, the damage in Damour was shown widely. However, no one explained that its Christian population was massacred, its survivors were exiled and its homes were destroyed by the PLO in 1976-77. No pictures were circulated of apartment complexes in other towns still standing due to the respect for property the Israelis showed, with only specific floors bombed to flush out PLO forces there. Nor was there any coverage of PLO brutalities such as extracting plasma from Lebanese civilians or using women as shields in battle.

The headlines blared: "Israeli Jets Shatter Mideast Cease-fire."

Many pages later, the small print read: "The strikes were in retaliation for seventy-five Arab truce violations." Reporters parroted inflated casualty figures due to the Israeli drive. But no one mentioned the 25,000 Syrians killed by Syrian soldiers in Hama, Syria, several months before. They also neglected to mention the 800 Lebanese killed and 3,000 wounded by the Syrian "peacekeeping forces" and the nearly 100,000 Lebanese killed during the PLO oppression. In fact, if Israel had not opened its borders to the Lebanese Christians for both medical aid and employment and had not helped them fight the PLO, there might not have been any Christians in southern Lebanon today. But nobody reported that.

Why such a blatant double standard not only in media coverage, but also in international diplomacy? A group of Christian scholars meeting in western Vermont in October 1982 made a suggestion. They noted that people who stood silent for years about various mass slaughters in the Middle East and elsewhere loudly condemned Israel about the massacre in West Beirut. On the other hand, there was little criticism at all of the Christian militia that engaged in the slaughter. The study group concluded: "The history of anti-Semitism demonstrates that the world has too often remained silent in the face of atrocities except where Israel stands accused."

The Palestinian Massacre

One of the situations where Israel has been most bitterly accused, and condemned, was for the September 1982 slaughter of Palestinians in two refugee camps by the Lebanese Christian militia, in retaliation for the assassination of President-elect Bashir Gemayel and his advisers. While most of world opinion lashed out at Israel as the culprit, U.S. Ambassador to the UN Jeanne Kirkpatrick pointed out, "Moral responsibility for the heinous massacre deserves to be divided among quite a large number of parties. The initial responsibility—moral, legal and political—lies with the people who did the killing. Beyond that the moral responsibility lies with all those parties who didn't do what they could do to maintain order and security." These include the United States, France, Italy (the countries who had sent in peacekeeping troops and then pulled them out—apparently too soon), Lebanon and Israel. She also named the PLO, Soviet Union and Cuba as those who inflamed the situation and actively supported the unrest. The Lebanese Christians who did the killing deserve blame. So do those Israelis who might have been able to prevent it. So also do the PLO (and their allies, the leftist Lebanese Muslims, and their suppliers in the Soviet bloc and Arab world). The Palestinians destroyed a country they had no right to be in. As others have further observed, Saudi Arabia, Jordan, Syria, Iraq, Egypt and the other Arab countries share the responsibility as well. They persistently refused to take in their Arab brothers, and so helped create the Palestinian refugee situation.

In all the decades of Arab terrorism against Jews and against Israel—even after the murder of Israeli athletes at the Munich Olympics or the slaughter of children in Israeli nurseries—rarely has there been an official word of Arab sympathy. These events usually draw a response of Arab applause or silence, certainly not an official investigation. In stark contrast, in Israel ten per cent of the population demonstrated in the streets to show their outrage over the massacre and to demand official action. Further distinguishing herself from her neighbors and demonstrating a vigorous democracy at work, Israel has begun an official investigation into the massacre. At this writing the Lebanese government has not followed suit. Add to this the persistent investigative reporting of the Israeli press, and everyone can be sure that, as Vice President George Bush noted, "the truth is going to come out."

But once again, the double standard thrives. King Hussein, in a torrent of emotion and eloquence, blamed it all on the Israelis. Yet he never acknowledged that most of the people were in camps in the first place because he kicked them out of Jordan in a bloody war. As Commentary Editor Norman Podhoretz wrote, "In a morally sane climate responsibility would have been assigned to the thugs who initiated this particular cycle of murderous horrors and their opposite numbers who responded in barbarous kind. . . . But when Christians murdered Moslems for having murdered Christians, the world immediately began denouncing the Jews who were, at the very worst, indirectly involved." He concluded, "Here again the old double standard made another ugly appearance. And with this new failure to distinguish among relative weights of responsibility, our public discourse has taken another great slide down the slippery slope to moral idiocy."[37]

Causes of the Conflict

What has caused the Mideast conflict? The age-old animosity of Ishmael, the father of the Arabs, toward Isaac, the ancestor of the Jews, plays some part (see Gen 21:8-10). Ishmael wanted the inheritance and blessings that Abraham passed on to Isaac. That inheritance included the land of Israel. But there is more to it. Is it the occupied territories? The conflict existed before Israel occupied the territories in 1967. From the beginning, in 1948, the Arabs made no movement toward peace; they directed their efforts toward war. Is it the refugee problem? Again, the conflict existed before the refugees. All those who left Israel in 1948 left by choice, at the urging of Arab leaders and despite the pleas of Israeli officials. Is it the lack of a Palestinian state? In 1948 Israel accepted the UN resolution partitioning Palestine into the Jewish and Palestinian Arab states. The Arabs rejected this and began the war. From 1948 to 1967, with Palestinian lands under Egyptian and Jordanian control, no one called for a Palestinian state.

These are not the real issues. The conflict's roots go deeper. The attempts to present the conflict as religious or military, as in the Zionism-racism UN resolution, simply reflect the Arabs' basic intransigence. They refuse to recognize the reality of a Jewish peoplehood and national entity with its own language, culture and history, its own social, economic and political structure.

This refusal and hostility has a long history, from the Islamic conquest of the Holy Land in 637—when the Arabs first made Jews second-class citizens—right through the twentieth century. In the 1880s, for example, while under Turkish rule, Jewish villages had to defend themselves against Arab marauding, murder and rape. Under British rule in 1920 came an upsurge in Arab assaults with the murderous assault on Tel Hai in Galilee and wild riots in Jerusalem. A year later an Arab mob attacked the Jewish quarter of Jerusalem, intent on slaughtering its inhabitants, and was barely repulsed. In 1929, a large portion of the Jewish inhabitants of Hebron were killed and most of the others driven out. In the years 1936-

39, the country was inundated with Arab attacks on Jews in cities and settlements alike as part of a campaign organized by the Mufti of Jerusalem. The Arabs' failure to recognize Israel's right to exist as a nation, and even earlier as a distinct people, lies at the root of the conflict.[38] This has resulted in the Arab failure to perceive the need for mutual relationships.

In fact, do the Arab governments seriously want peace in the Mideast? The facts seem to indicate otherwise, as the late Senator Hubert Humphrey pointed out.

1. No Arab nation has recognized Israel or has expressed a great willingness to do so.

2. No Arab nation has been willing to abandon the systematic scheme of boycott and diplomatic pressure on Israel.

3. No Arab leader [this should now be amended to read: "Only one Arab leader . . . "] has accepted Israel's invitation to come forward and negotiate directly.[39]

While the Israelis, particularly under the leadership of Menachem Begin, have been criticized as intransigent and inflexible, they have made the only tangible sacrifices for peace.[40] They gave up the Sinai, which had made them energy independent, militarily secure and economically healthy; and they did so, much to the pain and detriment of many of their own people. How have the Arab leaders (apart from Anwar Sadat) responded? Occasionally they issue nebulous statements such as the Arab League's response at Fez to President Reagan's peace initiative, which Western diplomats hurry to embrace as implicit recognition of Israel. Then they clarify their position, as Hani al-Hasan, an adviser to PLO chief Yasir Arafat, did in the Arabic language London newspaper Al-Hawadith. The Fez plan "does not mean recognition" of Israel, he said; it is a "tool for struggle and not for negotiation."[41]

Sometimes Arab leaders get together, as they did during the International Islamic Conference in January 1981, and demand that Jewish people get out of Israel. At this conference, the leader of the "moderates," Saudi Arabia, led the conference in calling for an Islamic holy war against Israel.

Arab leaders who pursue peace face different treatment. In 1979 village councils were created by people throughout most of the West Bank. The councils in turn established regional Village

Leagues to represent the moderate majority of West Bank residents. The Leagues seek to deal peaceably with Israel and have emerged as competition to PLO sympathizers. Rather than welcome this peaceful alternative, on March 9, 1982, Jordan's Prime Minister Mudar Badran issued a decree stating that any West Bank Arab associating with the Leagues "will be prosecuted for treason and will be brought before the competent court, which will pass the required sentences. The maximum penalty will be death and the confiscation of all immovable and movable properties."[42]

Rather than wait for such "justice," the PLO has bombed and assassinated League leaders. The assassination of President Anwar Sadat of Egypt in October 1981 serves as an excellent example of Arab attitudes toward peace. After his murder, none of the Arab leaders, including the "moderates," grieved. Many, including the PLO, celebrated in the streets. The rest blamed his death on his making peace with Israel. Yasir Arafat later said, "Whoever contemplates betraying his Arab nation as Sadat did, his fate will be bullets from the guns that just passed in front of us."[43] Shortly after his election and public statement favoring a peace treaty with Israel, the late President-elect of Lebanon, Bashir Gemayel, discovered how most Arabs react to peace initiatives with Israel. With his brutal assassination, the only two men in the Arab world to have attempted peace with Israel lay dead.

Christian Responsibility
In light of the issues, believers have certain responsibilities. If God's people show a concern for justice, as he expects, they cannot opt for neutrality and even-handedness. Committed Christians, without hating Arabs, must support Israel's struggle for survival and security. Regardless of whether or not you agree with an Israeli course of action, you will want to be as supportive as you possibly can, joining your Jewish friends in some of their efforts. Urge members of Congress and public officials to continue their support of Israel. Write letters to newspapers and magazines encouraging support for Israel and indicating why. Give financially to charitable Israeli organizations. Remember, Jewish people have a strong tie to Israel. By following these suggestions you demonstrate your concern for them and for Israel.

6

THE INFLUENCE OF TWO WARS

Two events significantly influenced recent Jewish perspectives, the Six-Day War of 1967 and the Yom Kippur War of 1973.[1] These wars had a strong impact on the Jewish community, especially among the youth. Very rapidly Israel's fate became much more important than the other causes they participated in. A number of occurrences emphasizing the aloneness and distinctiveness of the Jewish people triggered this response. These occurrences justified the Jews' right to consider themselves specially threatened and also highlighted the need for efforts to insure their survival.

The Impact of the Wars

First, Black and White activist groups responded antagonistically to Israel. Jewish people, especially the youth, had fought side by side with many of these groups for the same causes. During the Six-Day War many activists showed anti-Israel, pro-Arab attitudes. They denounced Israel as imperialistic, militaristic and racist. This conflicted with the Jewish people's love for Israel. Many Jews felt their friends had turned on them and left them alone in a time of crisis. Only Jews showed any concern for Jewish problems.

About this time also, ethnic groups copied the Blacks' emphasis on self-assertion. Irish-American, Polish-American and Italian-American became labels of pride and distinction. This helped to legitimize Jewish self-assertion and active support of Jewish interests, as Jews followed suit.

In 1967 the Soviet Union rose to prominence as one of Israel's major enemies as Soviet anti-Zionist propaganda reached new heights of intensity and absurdity. This forcefully brought the plight of three million Soviet Jews to the attention of the world Jewish community. Jews were more oppressed and deprived of their rights than almost any other people, solely because they were Jewish. This re-emphasized the aloneness and distinctiveness of Jewish people and again highlighted the need to insure their survival.

The rediscovery of the Holocaust probably contributed most to the Jewish people's new awareness. For many the Holocaust had become a fading memory. Jewish young people remained oblivious to the events that had brutally exterminated over half of Europe's Jewish population. The specter of the Holocaust was revived when Arab leaders promised to push the Jews into the sea. This raised the possibility of genocide once again. The world had stood by once before while Nazis liquidated Jews. The two wars indicated that things had not changed much.

> For two long weeks in May 1967 the worldwide Jewish community perceived the spectre of a second Jewish Holocaust in a single generation. For two weeks it listened to the same words emanating from Cairo and Damascus which had once emanated from Berlin. For two weeks it longed for Christian words of apprehension and concern. But whereas some such words came from secular sources, from the churches there was little but silence. Once again Jews were alone.[2]

The two wars, as well as the oil crisis and repeated hostile UN resolutions, demonstrated not only the isolation of the Jewish people but other nations' animosity toward them also. The Yom Kippur War provides an excellent example. Other nations expressed little alarm when the combined Arab armies attacked Israel on the most holy day of the Jewish year. They made no outcry when Arab armies overran Israeli defenses and threatened to crush Israel. Even the United States delayed its aid. The first sign of alarm occurred when the battle's tide changed and the Israeli army began advancing on Cairo and Damascus. Not until then did any nation attempt to stop the war. The world cared little for Jewish lives. However, they did show concern for the availability of Arab oil.

A number of events, therefore, highlighted the Jewish people's isolation and distinctiveness: the indifference of so many nations, the Arabs' avowed attempt to push Israel into the sea, the Soviet Jewish situation, and the activist response in the United States. These events also reinforced the lessons learned from the Holocaust. Therefore, many came to believe, any trust in Gentiles must be cautious and tentative at best; there is no certainty that what happened in Nazi Germany will not be repeated.

As a result of all these factors, Jewish survival achieved a deep, new significance. It had become God's command for the Jewish people, and they must make every effort to ensure it. So Jews insisted on being and remaining Jewish, and they repeated a familiar statement more frequently: "I was born a Jew and I'll die a Jew."

This new mood resulted in the formation of the militant Jewish Defense League. Its motto, "Never Again," referred directly to the Holocaust and similar attempts to kill off Jewish people. As another result of the new mood, Jewish people strenuously oppose anything that even appears to threaten their survival and identity.

What the victory [1967] did for us, and perhaps for most American Jews, was to reinforce a thousandfold a new determination to resist . . . any who would in any way and to any degree and for any reason whatsoever attempt to do us any harm, any who would diminish us or destroy us, any who would challenge our right and our duty to look after ourselves and our families, any who would deny us the right to pursue our own interests or frustrate us in our duty to do so.[3]

Correspondingly, concerned Jews intensified the attack on assimilation and the factors contributing to it. One writer described the new attitudes as "the commanding voice of Auschwitz" (one of the most notorious of Hitler's death camps, Auschwitz became a frequent symbol of the entire Holocaust program):

Jews are forbidden to grant posthumous victories to Hitler. They are commanded to survive as Jews, lest the Jewish people perish. They are commanded to remember the victims of Auschwitz, lest their memory perish. They are forbidden to despair of man and his world, and to escape in either cynicism or other-worldliness, lest they cooperate in the delivering the world over to the forces of Auschwitz. Finally, they are forbidden to despair of the God of Israel, lest Judaism perish. A secularist Jew cannot make himself believe by a mere act of the will, nor can he be commanded to do so; yet he can perform the commandment of Auschwitz, and a religious Jew who has stayed with his God may be forced into new, possibly revolutionary, relationships with him. One possibility, however, is wholly unthinkable. A Jew may not respond to Hitler's attempt to destroy Judaism by himself cooperating in its destruction. In ancient times, the unthinkable Jewish sin was idolatry. Today it is to respond to Hitler by doing his work.[4]

In the light of history a Jewish person simply cannot consider as a viable option anything which even remotely contributes to Judaism's breakdown.

The sense of aloneness and distinctiveness has not diminished in the decade since the two wars. The chairman of the Conference of Presidents of Major American Jewish Organizations, Theodore Mann, reflected the Jewish community's concern in an article called "Fighting the Big Lies":

A feeling of isolation, Jewish isolation, remarkably akin to the feelings that gripped world Jewry in May, 1967—that, too, is bothering me. . . . Israel is gradually being made a pariah among nations, and Jews are being made into criminals precisely as they were in Germany in 1935 (that is, through the "big lie"). . . . Have we as a Jewish community made the right judgments about what other Americans are really like? We have assumed, for example, that oil blackmail would be repugnant to most Americans, that succumbing to blackmail is simply not in the American character.

But statements from both sides of the political spectrum, under the guise of speaking in our economic best interests, indicate otherwise. So Mann goes on to say:

They have said it [that we should side with the Arabs solely because they provide us with oil] openly, unashamedly, precisely as if no moral issue even fits into the equation. . . . Have we altogether misjudged the mood and character of Americans?[5]

As might be expected, the Jewish community's concern for its survival and identity remains strong also. The rapid growth of the Havurah movement—religious home fellowships—clearly points in this direction. So does the continued popularity and repeated expansions of The Jewish Catalog, a practical guide to living Jewishly, the third volume of which was added to the series in 1982.

Key '73, an attempt to unify U.S. churches by calling the nation to commitment to God through Jesus, and other evangelistic campaigns, such as Here's Life America, have also contributed to the increased emphasis on Jewish survival and identity. Jews viewed Key '73 as an attempt by Christians to convert all non-Christians in the United States. This understanding assumes tremendous significance in view of the common Jewish perspective that all Gentiles are Christians unless they follow the Eastern religions. As one rabbi expressed it, "If the Christians want to convert the non-Christians in the United States, who does that leave to convert? Just us and the Buddhists." Thus, Jewish people view Key '73 and almost every active evangelistic effort as a specific attempt to convert Jews. And Jews cite conversion as one of the main causes of assimilation and a major threat to Jewish survival.

Often evangelism arouses a deeper fear, that evangelistic fervor will result in anti-Semitism. Unfortunately, history justifies this fear: evangelism has repeatedly resulted in persecution and oppression of Jewish people (see chapter four, "A Survey of Church-Synagogue Relations"). As Jews view it, things haven't changed. A prominent lecturer reflected this, "I am concerned that this evangelistic fervor will inevitably result in the children of Jewish converts to Christianity leading in the persecution of my children."[6] As one example of this, in 1390 Rabbi Solomon HaLevi converted to Christianity and became Bishop Don Pablo de Santa Maria. He turned out to be one of Spanish history's most hostile anti-Semites.[7]

Active evangelism, then, causes deep concern among many Jews. They fear it will result not only in all-out conversion attempts aimed specifically at them but also in anti-Semitism and persecution. They therefore view evangelism as the beginning of an attempt to wipe out Judaism. It threatens Jewish survival and identity, thus striking at the very heart of the new mood brought on by the two wars. A rabbi expressed this apprehension that evangelism "promotes a stifling, suppressive climate, intrudes on the privacy of Jews, plans their quick liquidation and extinction, and shelters anti-Semitism." Or to put it more bluntly, as one Jewish man did recently, "This mission business is just like murder; we might as well lose one to Hitler as to the Christians."

The Workings of God
In this time period since the wars, God has worked spiritually among the Jewish people in a significant fashion. In Israel, for example, several verified accounts of supernatural or providential events during the two wars have surfaced.[8] This has had its effect, as one Israeli observed: "The elements of the miraculous have not been lost on the nation. There is a strong feeling of deliverance from what mght have been a terrible catastrophe.... Stickers appeared on cars and busses with the slogan 'Israel, trust in God.' "[9]

Israeli public schools have always taught the Old Testament to all students. Just recently, however, the school system has launched a program to teach the life of Jesus and the Gospels to junior high students. God's Word will inevitably produce results (Is 55:11).

The American Jewish community shows similar signs of God's hand. In the last decade many Jewish people have expressed a growing spiritual hunger, an intense searching for God. A Jewish scientist reflected this: "The Jewish nature and soul needs to know God; it must be told about God. Our souls are looking for God and are trying to know God and no one has told them."[10] In addition, after an evaluation of the perilous nature of our times, some Jewish people now look and hope for a supernatural solution. One rabbi expressed it: "History is rushing to a close. God must intervene as He did in the time of Moses. This is the time when Messiah will come. He might even come tomorrow." These have become significant trends among Jewish people, but another important factor has also entered the picture.

Recently a growing number of Jews have accepted Jesus as

Messiah. This trend has alarmed many rabbis, some of whom have estimated that from two to three thousand Jewish people become believers every year. One rabbi's evaluation of this situation caused him to remark, appropriately but sarcastically: "We are living in an age where people want to touch, approach, and feel God. Judaism has always been very abstract. . . . [It] raises more questions than it answers. The Jesus movement has all the answers."[11]

And yet the permeation of Christianity with anti-Jewish sentiment makes it virtually impossible for most thinking Jewish people to consider it a serious option. This was forcefully brought home to my wife and me when an elderly Jewish woman told us: "What holds me back from accepting Jesus as Messiah are all the horrible things Christians have done to us. And they've done it time after time. For me it's an insurmountable wall." In addition, "Psychologically, Christianity is too intimately involved in Jewish minds with the guilt of the Holocaust for Jews to be able to speak or listen freely to it, and the silence of organized Christianity during the Six Day War has only increased those emotional barriers."[12]

Further, the hidden expectation that Jews who accept Jesus must abandon their Jewishness only compounds the problem. Because of this expectation Christianity has unwittingly, or perhaps wittingly, assisted in the elimination of the Jewish people. Under these conditions adherence to Christianity would mean Jewish people aiding in their own destruction. In his book *Faith after the Holocaust*, Rabbi Eliezer Berkovits summed it up in this way:

> Since the tree is to be judged by its fruits, the standards and values of this religion and civilization have become questionable. Christianity never really presented a serious spiritual challenge for the Jew. In view of the Christian performance through the ages, Christianity has never been as dead an option for the Jew as it is today.[13]

The Resolution of the Conflict

Two important trends, then, apparently stand in opposition to each other. On one hand, Jews are more open to Jesus' message. On the other, they strongly oppose evangelism and assimilation. Yet even here we can see God at work. In the early 1970s a solution to the tension between these trends emerged. Independently of one an-

other, congregations of Jewish (and Gentile) believers sprang up in
Jewish communities across the United States. Virtually no outside influence brought this about other than the leading of the Holy
Spirit and the Word of God. God apparently superintended this
grassroots movement to integrate the conflicting influences.

These congregations share a unique commitment: that they can
believe in Jesus and be thoroughly biblical as well as authentically
Jewish. The congregations affirm Jesus as Messiah, Savior and
Lord. They hold to the Old and New Testaments as the inspired
Word of God and accept no practice or teaching contradictory
to the Bible. They feel a oneness and commitment to Messiah's
entire body, yet they express their faith, lifestyle and worship in
Jewish ways and forms. They do not believe that this Jewish observance gives them special merit, blessing or spirituality before
God. It is just a delightful way to live and worship and maintain
their culture.

These congregations help to illustrate the unity of Messiah's
body. In 1 Corinthians 12 the apostle Paul warned that unity does
not equal uniformity but consists of harmony in diversity. A brief
survey of U.S. evangelicals yields many examples of this. Blacks,
Hispanics and Orientals express their faith, worship and lifestyle
in ways that uniquely fit their cultural backgrounds. Others worship in distinct denominational styles such as Baptist, Presbyterian or Lutheran. Yet they express their unity in the Messiah. M. G.
Bowler has effectively summarized this principle.

A homogenous mass of indistinguishable disciples would be
no proof of [the unity that is possible in the Messiah]. It is the
very fact that we see the differences alongside the unity that
proves to us that [the Messiah] does take diverse and normally anti-pathetic groups and individuals and unites them
in the deepest sense. He does this without the "melting" or
"welding" or other impersonal processes which a merely
institutional amalgamation would involve. The different are
still different but the diversity is that of an orchestra.... It
is when [believers] are noticeably different and yet noticeably
united that the full impact of [Messiah's] unifying work is mani-
fested.

[The Messiah] unites those who follow Him by drawing them

into union with Himself. . . . The New Covenant, of which [Messiah] is the mediator, forms a community which includes men and women of many different ethnic and cultural streams, and each can learn and profit from contact with his fellow who is also ["in Messiah"]. Male and female are one [in the Messiah] but this fact doesn't rob . . . marriage of its significance and content, because the natural difference remains in the partners to give meaning to the union. The Jew and the Gentile who are also ["one in Messiah"] also retain their respective identities or should. Paul doesn't testify as an ex-Jew. He refers to himself as . . . "a Jew" (Acts 21:39).[14]

The same thing happens in foreign countries. One basic purpose of communicating God's message to the people in these countries is to establish indigenous congregations. These express their faith in Jesus locally in ways relevant and meaningful to the people of the native culture. This principle is not new. Years ago Hudson Taylor went to China to communicate the biblical message there. He shaved his head and grew a pigtail, wore Chinese clothes, ate Chinese food and used chopsticks, living in a Chinese way among the Chinese people. Many considered him a radical, but he didn't actually try anything new. He merely followed Paul's example (1 Cor 9:19-23). Paul proclaimed that, to communicate Jesus' message effectively, he lived as a Jew among Jews, under the law (the Jewish traditions) among those under the law. He provided a living demonstration that a person could be Jewish and believe in Jesus. So today, Jewish (and Gentile) believers are forming themselves into local congregations or synagogues in Jewish communities. They express their faith in Jesus and affirm their Jewishness while being thoroughly biblical. They therefore demonstrate that Jews can maintain their identity and ensure their survival while following Jesus. The congregations, then, help resolve the tension between Jewish openness to Jesus' message and Jewish resistance to evangelism and assimilation.

Some people may view the Messianic Jewish movement as something new. Perhaps it is new for our generation, but it is really very old. The movement has merely returned to a New Testament pattern. After all, Jesus and all his early followers lived as Jews. Jesus kept the Jewish customs and taught other Jews to do the same (Mt

5:17-19; 23:3; Jn 8:46; Gal 4:4). Excited about the beauty and meaning of their traditions as seen in the light of Jesus and his mission (Lk 24:47; Mt 5:17), the apostles continued to observe the Jewish customs: worshiping in the Temple, keeping the festivals, making the ceremonial vows and undergoing purification (Acts 2:46-47; 18:18; 20:5-6, 16; 21:20-26; 27:9; 1 Cor 7:18). In fact, in the last passage Paul expressly instructed Jewish believers to maintain their practices and identity. His life and statements illustrate his commitments. Not only did he follow the Jewish traditions, even making a public demonstration of his devotion to them (Acts 21:20-26), he based his defense before both Gentile and Jewish officials on his consistent observance (Acts 25:8; 28:17). Before the Jewish religious court, he went so far as to claim that he had lived strictly as a Pharisee (a sect that strictly observed Jewish traditions) and *still* continued that lifestyle, as the tense of the Greek verb in Acts 26:5 indicates.

History reinforces the biblical picture of the apostles' Jewish lifestyle. The historian Josephus reports the martyrdom of James, Jesus' brother, at the instruction of the high priest.[15] This incensed the Pharisees so much that they complained to Rome and had the high priest removed. They held James in such high esteem because he had lived a consistent, godly, Jewish life. Irenaeus, an important second-century church leader whose teacher Polycarp was taught by the apostles, reflected on the apostles' lifestyle: "They themselves continued in the ancient observances. . . . Thus did the apostles scrupulously act according to the dispensation of the Mosaic law."[16]

What were the results of Jesus' and the apostles' preaching the message from within a Jewish context? Thousands of Jewish people accepted Jesus as the Messiah (Acts 2:41; 4:4; 6:7; 21:20). Today's Messianic movement is attempting to follow this example.

The movement has experienced some thrilling results. Gentiles in the Messianic synagogues are excited about discovering the roots of their faith. They have been enriched by seeing the significance of many biblical passages as viewed through Jewish eyes. They have seen that many Jewish practices provide beautiful visual illustrations of important biblical truths. The Bible has come alive for them as a result of their new-found Jewish insights. They have fully integrated themselves into congregational life, even as far as taking leadership roles in some cases.

The Messianic synagogues have also provided the church with a valuable service. They have served as an example as well as a stimulus to help Christians understand and recapture their Jewish roots. Because roots are important to the faith, Paul reminded the Roman believers of their own roots (Rom 11:17-18; 9:4-5; see also Eph 2:11-13). As a foremost evangelical leader put it: "There is something shallow about a Christianity that has lost its Jewish roots."

A prominent rabbi's observation summarizes another result of the Messianic movement. "In the past, Jews who have [become believers in Jesus] were largely on the periphery of Jewish life. A large percentage were cranks and crackpots. Now it is quite different."[17] The mainstream of the Jewish community is much more ready to come to the Messianic synagogues. Here they see recognizable Jewish things, yet can perceive the difference due to the life, reality and fulfillment available through faith in Jesus. And they hear the New Testament message as well as the Old. As a result they are more willing to hear about Jesus and the atonement he provides. In effect they go back in time to the first-century biblical Jewish setting; they return to the way Jesus and the apostles worshiped.

Messianic synagogues have the potential for communicating God's message to entire Jewish families and neighborhoods as never before. At one West Coast Messianic synagogue eighty Jewish people trusted Jesus in eighteen months; an East Coast synagogue experienced similar growth. In Chicago a young Jewish woman accepted Jesus several years ago and became concerned for her parents. Her parents consistently refused to attend church or Christian functions with her. Finally they attended a Messianic synagogue and a few weeks later trusted Jesus.

But to achieve this full potential requires effort. Not only must the synagogue members demonstrate a life and reality found only in the Messiah, they must prove their authentic and consistent Jewishness. Then they can effectively answer objections such as these:

There is little evidence that modern Jewish Christians are as Jewishly observant as their ancient counterparts. We find among them that Hebrew is limited, Kashrut [observing kosher dietary traditions] rare, and Jewish liturgy unusual. Admittedly, this may also be the case among "unfulfilled" Jews but somehow the embracing of "that man" represents the final straw.[18]

Despite all their pious declarations, they have abandoned the Jewish faith and the Jewish people. These deserters have walked out on the period of our greatest martyrdom and on our greatest time of redemption. How dare they claim that they are still Jews when they have cast aside every shred of responsibility, every duty, every mitzva of Jewish life? Compounding their betrayal is their phoniness.[19]

For a variety of reasons some Jewish people may not want to worship in a Jewish setting and so would be uncomfortable in a Messianic synagogue. However, the vast majority, even the nonreligious, will be attracted to it; the Messianic synagogue is not just for the Orthodox or the devout Jew. As one nonreligious young man put it after visiting a Messianic synagogue, "Now I can definitely see that you can be Jewish and believe in Jesus." He accepted Jesus as Messiah shortly thereafter and found a home in that congregation. For 89% of the Jewish people, being Jewish is important; 83% feel that religious aspects play an important part in Jewish identity.[20] The many Jewish people who are concerned about Jewish survival and Jewish identity need the environment Messianic synagogues provide; they need this environment for their own growth as well as for the effectiveness of their testimony before their family and neighbors.

An evaluation of the time since the Six-Day War definitely leads to the conclusion that God works in ways beyond human understanding and explanation (Rom 11:33-34). He sometimes does this as a specific reminder to us not to put him in a box or restrict the manner in which he might choose to accomplish his purpose. A number of years ago few people thought that Jews would accept Jesus on such a large scale as they now do, and very few could have imagined anything similar to the Messianic Jewish movement as God's agent. Yet God brought it about.

Because God's ways are often mysterious, many well-meaning

people criticize movements brought into being by God. As a result, allegations and distortions have a heyday; misunderstandings abound. I wrote the following open letter to try to clear away just such misunderstandings and distortions.[21]

An Open Letter

My Brothers and Sisters,

In recent months a lot has been said and written about a "new and different" thing that is happening among Jewish people who have become followers of Jesus the Messiah. I'm referring to that movement of people who speak of themselves as Messianic Jews, who believe that it is perfectly consistent to maintain their identity as Jews while being committed to Jesus as Savior and Lord. Due to the very nature of the people and the movement, a number of misconceptions have surfaced and a number of Christians have become alarmed.

I am a Messianic Jew and I'm concerned. I'm concerned about you and about your apprehensions about me and others like me. I'm concerned that I and other Messianic Jews not misrepresent ourselves and that we not be misunderstood. So please, allow me to tell you more about myself and others like me.

I didn't always consider myself a Messianic Jew; I didn't always understand how my Jewish identity related to my faith in Jesus. For a time I thought I had to totally set aside my Jewish identity. It was only after much biblical study and consideration that I came to the position I now hold. Many in this movement have gone through the same struggle that I have gone through before coming to their present convictions. And yet, many others had to struggle very little in coming to terms with their present identity.

Do you find it so strange that we are asking you to allow us to keep our Jewish identity and culture? Don't you allow Americans to remain Americans when they trust Jesus? Do you ask the Chinese to stop being Chinese when they become believers? So why should we be the only ones who aren't allowed to be ourselves?

"But doesn't the Bible teach, 'There is neither Jew nor Greek' (Gal 3:28)?" you might ask. Most certainly physical distinctions have no bearing on our relationship with God. Yet that same verse goes on to say, "There is neither male nor female." There are few who would maintain that the male-female distinction has been set aside, especially since the Bible maintains the distinctions in a number of ways. In the same way the Bible does recognize a distinctness between Jews and Gentiles. Witness Paul's references to himself in Acts 22:3, Romans 11 and 2 Corinthians 11. He doesn't speak as a non-Jew. Speaking about our unity or oneness in the Messiah, M. G. Bowler points out that unity does not mean uniformity (p. 84). Paul also makes this quite clear in 1 Corinthians 12. The whole body doesn't consist of an eye (uniformity); if it did, the body wouldn't exist. The one body has many different members (unity). This makes for harmony in the diversity, whether that diversity is Presbyterian, Baptist, Lutheran or Jewish.

Does this Jewish emphasis separate Jewish and Gentile believers, thus erecting the so-called middle wall of partition? Absolutely not. We will have no part in such exclusiveness. Gentile Christians are completely welcome to participate with us in every way, and they do so. In fact some of the most excited people among us are Gentiles who have been enriched by seeing the significance of many biblical practices as highlighted by the Jewish customs. They have said that they have seen the Bible "come alive" for them. Further, in many of our congregations, Gentile believers have become part of our leadership as well as our membership.

Is this Judaizing? According to Galatians, Judaizing involved teaching others, especially Gentiles, that they had to observe the entire Jewish system in order to be saved or to be properly spiritual. In other words, observing the system would result in merit before God or in greater spirituality or blessing. We steadfastly oppose all such teaching. Observing the Jewish customs and ceremonies will never result in salvation, blessing, spirituality or merit. Gentiles are not told they must become Jews, and people are not told that they must observe the customs.

But in writing against Judaizing, Paul does not condemn the observance of Jewish customs. Alan Cole, a foremost evangelical scholar, makes this quite clear in *The Epistle of Paul to the Galatians*:

> Again there seems to be here a recognition that it is possible for the church of God to be one without being uniform in cus-

tom, habit or sphere. Paul never seems to have compelled the Gentile Churches to act like Jews. . . . But it remains equally true that he does not expect Jewish Churches to act like Gentile believers; he never says that it is wrong for them to be circumcised or to keep the law, or to observe the festivals. All he insists is that these things have nothing to do with the gift of salvation. Not only so, but there is a glad recognition of differences of sphere appointed by God![22]

We believe that we have the freedom to observe the Jewish practices (Gal 4:4; Acts 2; 18; 20; 21; et al.). In fact, the early faith and practices of the followers of Jesus were so Jewish that for a short while there was a question as to whether a person could be a believer in Jesus without being or becoming Jewish (Acts 15)!

Why would anyone want to observe the Jewish practices? They are beautiful visual illustrations to help us understand all that God has done in history for us, and especially what he has done for us in Jesus the Messiah. When God instituted them in the Old Testament, and when he providentially superintended their development by the Jewish people, he intended these practices to convey spiritual truth. They enable us to visualize and experience the truths of God. The Jewish people, as part of their strong reverence for God and history, have preserved many of these enlightening practices virtually intact from times that even predate the Savior. Phil Goble, in *Everything You Need to Grow a Messianic Synagogue,* expresses it:

The Jewish festivals foreshadow the Messiah and are fulfilled in Him. However, a shadow cannot highlight anyone, even the Messiah, if it is totally removed from the picture. The Jewish festivals are not obsolete but are good contemporary teachers that point us toward the . . . New Covenant. . . . Jewish ceremony will be . . . pleasing in God's sight if done in the name of the One in whom all Jewish ceremonies are fulfilled (cf. Rom 14:3, 5; Acts 21:20-26).[23]

This is why Hebrews warns us not to go back to Judaism *apart from Jesus.* It can't be done. Jesus stands as the fulfillment of the Old Testament faith and practice, and apart from him that faith and practice has no meaning; it is an empty shell missing its life and reality. In him it reaches its highest expression. This is the meaning of Jesus' words in Matthew 5:17, where the idea being conveyed by the word *fulfill* is "to make complete, to bring to full expression."[24] The meaning is set in direct opposition to the idea of "to end or annul." The thrust of Matthew 5:17 permeates the message of Hebrews, where Jesus is seen as the crown of the Jewish system. He heightens and highlights it, bringing out its beauty and giving it meaning, taking it up in himself and making it complete. This is a very lofty view, as B. F. Westcott, one of the most outstanding evangelical scholars of the last century, attests:

> Prominence is assigned in the Epistle to the Old Testament, both to the writing and to the institutions which it hallows. There is not the least tendency towards disparagement of the one or the other. From first to last it is maintained that God spoke to the fathers in the prophets. The message through the Son takes up and crowns all that had gone before.[25]

Does this mean that Jewish people can get to God or receive salvation apart from faith in Jesus? Of course not! Paul makes this absolutely clear in Romans 1:16, and in chapter 3 as well. No person, whether Jew or Gentile, can approach God apart from the death and resurrection of Jesus. Salvation can come to a person, whether Jew or Gentile, only by grace through faith in Jesus. This is our consistent teaching and message.

Further, let me add that we have no quarrel with the existing churches. We don't feel that they are wrong or that we are better. We love them. And we have no quarrel with those who refer to themselves as Hebrew Christians. If believers find the term meaningful and comfortable, they should use the term but should also allow others to speak of themselves as Messianic Jews, Jews who are Messianists,[26] followers of Jesus the Messiah.

Make no mistake. We are committed to:

1. The Old and New Testaments as the inspired and authoritative Word of God;

2. Almighty God as a unique, composite unity of three persons;

3. Jesus as the only Savior, promised Messiah and Lord of the universe;

4. Salvation only by grace through faith in Jesus;

5. The body of the Messiah in both its universal and local expressions.

I'm concerned, as are the others who are part of this movement of Messianic Jews, that Jewish people all over the world come to know Jesus as Messiah and that his message go out unhindered. But I'm also concerned that brothers and sisters in the Messiah not jeopardize the work of others by way of denunciation and accusation; this is unscriptural (Rom 14:3-4, 10-13).

Many years ago in another country, a wise man faced a situation which caused him some doubt and alarm. A group of people claimed to be speaking a message from God. In a number of ways they had already demonstrated that their message was indeed from God, yet he had some lingering doubts. He gave this advice to those who listened: "Do not interfere with these men; for if this counsel or this work be of men, it will come to nothing. But if it be of God, you cannot overthrow it; and you may even find yourself fighting against God" (Acts 5:38-39).

7
PRINCIPLES OF COMMUNICATING THE BIBLICAL MESSAGE

Effective communication requires sensitivity toward the respondent and his background. That is why in previous chapters we have surveyed various areas important for understanding Jewish people. With this background material in mind, we need to learn how to relate to the respondent himself.

Eliminate Misconceptions and Stereotypes
Since misconceptions and stereotypes hinder communication, the first principle of sharing the biblical message is to eliminate them.

One common stereotype identifies things such as Jewish looks, characteristics or speech patterns. Someone might say, "He looks Jewish," or claim, "You can recognize a Jew by _____." People fill in the blank with a variety of descriptions. These statements contain an element of truth but many misunderstandings as well. Actually, quite a few so-called Jewish characteristics correspond to Mediterranean characteristics in general, and many people share them. A large number of Jews originated from the areas bordering the Mediterranean Sea and so have characteristics in common with other Mediterranean peoples: Italians, French, Spaniards, Greeks, Turks and Arabs. Further, many other "Jewish" mannerisms are really Eastern European, and thus are shared with the people of these countries where Jewish people lived for many centuries.

Several years ago when the oil crisis first arose, Newsweek did a cover story on it. The magazine cover illustrated the problem by showing an Arab in typical costume standing next to a gasoline pump with his hand around the hose, squeezing it shut. As it turned out, the Jewish cover photographer had had great difficulty finding an Arab to pose for him, so he did the next best thing: he put on the Arab clothes and posed for himself. No one knew the difference. The Mediterranean characteristics shared by Jews and Arabs made this possible.

Further, if you selected a random group of Jewish people from the United States, in that group you would find a number of blue-eyed blondes and freckle-faced redheads. Some Jews just do not have the Mediterranean characteristics. They share common characteristics with others from the place of their national origin, whether it be South America, Northern Europe or Asia. The story is told of an American Jewish delegation that recently visited the People's Republic of China. As part of their visit they spent time with the Chinese Jewish community. One of the first statements the Chinese Jewish delegates reportedly made to the American Jews was, "You don't look very Jewish." The Jews of today are truly a people from many ethnic, cultural and racial backgrounds.

Another common misconception is that all Jewish people share the same beliefs. Judaism is simply not that homogeneous. Several branches of belief systems exist within religious Judaism. The Orthodox hold strictly to the Jewish laws and traditions. Conservative Judaism affirms the authority of Jewish law and seeks to conserve tradition. But it also holds that Judaism needs to make changes to adapt to modern conditions. However, these changes must be made from within the framework of Jewish law and tradition. By contrast, Reform Judaism rejects final authority and final form. It retains only those elements of Jewish law and tradition which are "elevating, appropriate or meaningful" to modern man. The Reconstructionists, conceiving of Judaism in natural rather than supernatural terms, believe that it must be reconstructed to meet the conditions of today's world. To do this they integrate Judaism with naturalistic philosophy. In addition to these major religious varieties, smaller subgroups exist, such as the Traditionalists and the Hasidim. And of course, Messianic Jews should also be considered among the religious Jews.

Beyond these religious groupings many Jewish people are simply nonreligious: atheists, agnostics, secularists or religiously unaffiliated. Further, Sephardic Jews differ from Ashkenazi Jews. The Sephardic Jews lived in Southern Europe, North Africa and the Muslim countries, while Ashkenazi Jews lived in Northern, Western and Eastern Europe. Because of geographical and historical differences, different traditions arose.

One can therefore fairly conclude that all Jewish people will agree on virtually no stated doctrine.

Judaism cannot be a creedal religion and that for three reasons. ... First, if Judaism has dogmas, where are they? Why, for example, did the Sanhedrin during seven hundred years of spiritual predominance never publish a set of articles of Jewish faith? Second, no draft of the Jewish creed attempted by any individual has ever won universal acceptance, not even the Thirteen Principles of Faith drawn up by Moses Maimonides. ... Every article has been challenged by someone or other, and more than an occasional Orthodox Jew is a critic of it today. Third, Jews cannot share a set of dogmas for the very simple but compelling reason that they have never been of one mind on theological matters.[1]

A familiar saying circulates among Jewish people that if you ask two Jews a question, you will get three different answers and at least two more questions.

If Jewish people differ like this, then what makes up Jewishness? Actually, the differences should not be overemphasized. Fewer differences exist than things held in common, and the differences remain "family" differences. Jewishness, however, consists of many elements: sociological, cultural, ethnic, religious, national, racial, historical, psychological and intellectual. The strength and mixture of these elements varies from person to person. This variety, therefore, makes Jewishness elusive to define. Perhaps the Jews of the world are best described as a large community of people undergirded by a strong set of traditions. Many Christians think of most Jews as highly religious or devout. This is not the case. Approximately 55% of the American Jewish community does not actively affiliate itself with any synagogue. Only 30% attend synagogue as frequently as once a month or more.[2] While a significant portion of the youth appear to be moving toward a more traditional expression of their faith, many Jewish people have simply set religion aside. The beliefs and practices may appear irrelevant and irrational to them, or perhaps even outmoded. Some may feel that modern man has gone beyond this stage, while others have not found satisfaction, meaning and fulfillment in their observances. Many cannot hold to their traditional perspectives in light of the utter devastation the Holocaust produced.

Therefore, the average Jewish person does not qualify as a walking encyclopedia of the Old Testament. Although many Jews studied Old Testament as part of their early religious training, most have forgotten much of this training. Although the more traditional synagogues will read through much of the Old Testament on a yearly basis, the average person will not have accumulated a significant knowledge because of his sporadic or infrequent attendance. If he has forgotten some of his Hebrew training, he faces another problem. The synagogue reads Scripture in Hebrew. In fact, many Jewish people do not know what books the Old Testament contains.

Similarly, most Jews are not experts on the Messiah. In fact, not all Jewish people expect a Messiah. Reform Jews, for example, expect a Messianic age and not a person. Many Jewish people hold no Messianic concept at all. Even those who expect a Messiah view him differently than Christians. The Messiah will come to rule the earth in peace and justice, and all men will know God. Messiah has little or nothing to do with spiritual salvation. While he may be superhuman, he is not divine. Most Jewish people are not familiar with Isaiah 53, the major biblical Messianic passage. Therefore, Jewish people have not really rejected Jesus' Messiahship; they are ignorant of it. For example, several summers ago a friend talked to an eighty-four-year-old Jewish man in Chicago. As they conversed, our friend discovered that this man had never heard the claims of Jesus as the Jewish Messiah! He shared Jesus' message, and the Jewish man trusted Jesus as his Messiah.

Make Jewish People Your Friends

A second principle of communicating the message is that personal contacts are vital. The communicator must constantly be aware of the essentials of good communication as they relate to Jewish people.

First, demonstrate love and friendliness. Remember that the Jewish person knows the history of Christian persecution of Jews. Through your conversation, and especially your actions, show that you love him and his people, that Jesus' followers do love Jewish people. (In fact, believers should be known as the Jews' best friends, especially in view of their debt to the Jewish people: your Bible, Savior and salvation have come from the Jews.) Be a real friend; have a meaningful relationship with him. Do things together. Demonstrate your love, because actions mean more than words.

Tact, as well as honesty, is essential. Therefore, show a regard for his opinions and demonstrate your acceptance of him as a Jew, as part of the people chosen by God. Tell him that you hold sacred the words of his ancient prophets. Let him know that you admire the noble qualities of the Jewish people, such as their strong family life and high ethical values. Express your condemnation of and regret over Gentile persecution of Jews. *But express such sentiments only if you mean them!*

It is important to be interested in your Jewish friend's beliefs and opinions. Effective communication is never one-sided. Ask your friend to share his beliefs; it will help you get to know him. Ask specific questions about his religious practices and about Judaism. This is a good opportunity for you to learn more about Judaism; use it well. Also, take the time to express appreciation for aspects of your faith that come from Judaism.

Show interest and sympathy about the Jewish community's concerns. This may require wide reading so that you can be conversant in matters of interest to Jewish people, such as Jewish survival, anti-Semitism, the Mideast situation, assimilation, and oppression of Jewish minorities. Your reading might include publications such as the *Jerusalem Post, Jewish Press, Jewish Post and Opinion, Commentary,* and *Judaism.* It's important to be conversant, but it is important to be sympathetic as well.

An awareness of significant cultural influences is another essential that makes for effective communication. The Jewish community attaches a great deal of importance to education. The emphasis often results in independent thinking and also a liberal outlook socially, economically and politically. Therefore, what they perceive as a lack of independent thinking in many Christian circles amazes many Jews. Their open-mindedness makes it difficult for them to accept anything as exclusive as Jesus' "one-way" message. Jewish people tend toward an openness and frankness that surprises many Christians, who often interpret it as bluntness and aggressiveness. In reality, it is more of an earthiness or particular type of warmth. Occasionally coupled with this is an aura of "warm" sophistication which people often take as condescension. Actually, this also is part of that openness that Jewish people express as you get to know them better.

The Jewish community reflects other significant cultural influences. Owing to their strong emphasis on justice and concern for the oppressed, Jewish people tend to throw themselves wholeheartedly into causes they view as worthwhile. These may be humanitarian, social or political. A great majority of Jews are also taught to be peace-loving. Golda Meir's statement to the Arab nations expresses it best: "We can forgive you for killing our sons, but we cannot forgive you for forcing us to kill yours." As the statement implies, while Jewish people are peace-loving, they will defend themselves and their rights if challenged.

What Not to Say
Language use to a great extent determines effective communication. Arguing is obviously detrimental, as is also anything that conveys condescension or a "know-it-all" attitude. Certain words or phrases simply do not communicate. More precisely, they communicate the wrong concepts or feelings. Certain pat phrases or

traditional theological terms carry important meaning for Christians. However, they create confusion and misunderstanding when heard by those outside Christian circles. Remember, a person interprets what he hears in terms of his own frame of reference and background. So to some people *saved* refers to something done at the store or bank, and *born again* implies reincarnation.

Other terms, in addition to being totally misunderstood, also stir up strong negative images and feelings. The word *Christ* (a title, not Jesus' last name) takes on this role. It has no real Jewish connotation. Often Jewish people connect it with the phrase *Christ-killer.* While growing up in the United States, numbers of Jews heard this phrase while groups of kids throwing rocks and bottles chased them through the streets. And some people still taunt Jewish people with it today. The title *Christ* simply transliterates the Greek *Christos,* "Messiah." Therefore, "Jesus Christ the Messiah" is redundant.

Since Messiah is a good biblical, Jewish term, it is quite appropriate to refer to Jesus as Messiah. But remember, your Jewish friend's concept of Messiah may differ from yours. Jesus' contemporaries called him by his Hebrew name, *Yeshua.* Remember, they did not speak English but Hebrew, Greek and Aramaic (a language similar to Hebrew). You may have to explain your meaning when you first use *Yeshua,* but use of his Hebrew name will emphasize not only Yeshua's Jewishness but also his relevance and importance to Jewish people.

Another set of terms open to great misunderstanding and immense negative response includes *convert* and *conversion.* A Jewish story helps illustrate this:

A Jew converted and became a Catholic (or was it a Greek Orthodox?) Christian. Then it was noised that his conversion was not sincere, for on Fridays the neighbors smelled cooked chicken instead of fish. The priest went to investigate. He burst suddenly into the home of the "converted Jew," lifted the lid and behold it was chicken indeed.

"Now what do you have to say in your defense? Didn't I baptize you and tell you that you are no longer a Jew, but now you are a Christian and have to abide by the rules of the Church and not by the Torah and Talmud?"

"Yes indeed, dear Father," the new convert protested. "But I
did with the chicken like you did with me. Before I put it into
the pot, I sprinkled it and said, 'I baptise you.... You are no
longer chicken; from now on you are fish.' "[3]
The story is set in a time when under great pressure Jews converted
and took Gentile names to demonstrate their break with Judaism.
Informers spied on converts' homes to make sure they did not
celebrate the Sabbath, eat Jewish food or recite the Jewish blessings. If the new converts failed in any of these ways, they faced
punishment, torture and even death. The Inquisition nourished
this mind set. "Converted Jew" carries with it this historical and
emotional baggage.

Perhaps an illustration will convey some of the emotional impact that the terms *convert* and *conversion* have for Jewish people.
Imagine being a plantation owner in the deep South before the
Civil War. Someone tells you that in order to follow God properly
you must become a Negro slave. Or, suppose you're a black militant in Watts, and someone says you must become a white man
in order to get right with God. The feelings that would boil inside
are almost as strong as those a Jewish person usually feels when
you talk of conversion. Jews equate those terms with a complete
change of identity, culture and heritage. They imply the loss of all
Jewishness and becoming a Gentile. And, through the years, they
have meant force, threats and death for Jews as part of the process.

In fact, *convert* does not best translate the biblical Hebrew and
Greek terms, as many modern translations attest. The original lan-
guages convey the idea of *return* or *repent*. These more effectively
communicate the biblical concepts to Jewish people.

The terms *Christian* and *Christianity* also invariably communicate the wrong thing to Jews. They usually perceive as Christian
anyone who is not Jewish or not following an Eastern religion. The
term is virtually equivalent to *Gentile*. Therefore, almost all non-
Jews in the Western world are Christians. Multitudes of these
"Christians" have persecuted Jews through the centuries (see
chapter four, "A Survey of Church-Synagogue Relations"). This
has caused an understandable reaction on the part of Jewish people.

When stake and rack and wheel were tried to convert the Jew, he
identified the missionaries with the Christ whom they professed.

When expulsion or death were constant companions of Jewish fate, the cross became, to the Jew, a symbol of harsh persecution rather than love. In time, Jesus meant agony and fear—and therefore, the less said and heard of him the better. This comes as a shock to Christians who hear or read of it for the first time. How could the sweet, gentle face of Jesus evoke anything but the ardour of love and devotion? Yet such is the reality of history: cruelty has begotten rejection and silence.[4]

One rabbi described this situation well: "Christianity speaks so loud one can hardly hear the voice of its founder."[5]

Recently an evangelical seminary president visited Israel. While there he asked an Israeli, "What does the term *Christian* bring to your mind?" Without any hesitation the Israeli replied, "The Crusades, the Inquisition, and Nazi Germany." Add to this the fact that George Habash, leader of a terrorist group more violent than the PLO, identifies himself as an Arab Christian, and when he claims credit for terrorist activities in Israel he is usually identified as an Arab Christian. His identity as an Arab Christian—though certainly not in the New Testament sense—links terrorism to the cause of Christianity. The terms *Christian* and *Christianity* then grossly miscommunicate. They distort the message believers seek to convey to Jews. They communicate concepts and ideas contrary to what is intended. Yeshua's early followers rarely used the terms (only three times in the New Testament). They found other terms more accurate or descriptive. Their example bears repeating.

Unfortunately, most Jewish people consider the New Testament a non-Jewish book. In fact, many label it anti-Semitic. When you use it (and remember the early believers conveyed God's message very effectively without having the New Testament), point out that it was written by Jewish authors, concentrates on a Jew (Yeshua), and contains Jewish teachings. You may want to emphasize the relevance of the New Testament to Jewish people by using its Hebrew title *B'rit Hadashah* (pronounced *breet khah-dah-shah*). Correspondingly, Jews often call the Old Testament the *Tenach* (pronounced *tə-nock*). Use of the term *Old Testament* might cause a different problem to surface. A professor of Jewish studies put it this way: "When Christians use the term *Old Testament*, they do so to indicate it is no longer relevant and has been replaced." Terms such as *Torah, Older Testament* or *first half of Scripture* can be good substitutes.

The term *missionary*, like others already discussed, communicates many wrong ideas. One common Jewish definition describes a missionary as "someone out to steal our children, who bribes people to get baptized, and uses force and threats to get results." A well-known Jewish scholar throws additional light on this Jewish understanding. "The missionary is seen as pernicious for he forces the Jew to relive the history of his martyrdom, all the while pressing the claim that in approaching the Jew he does so out of love. What kind of love is it, Jews wonder, that would deprive a man of his heritage."[6]

In view of these perspectives it is best not to use a term which is so badly misconstrued. Yeshua's early followers got along without the term. Evangelicals should be able to sacrifice it for the sake of good communication with Jewish people.

One final term hinders communication with Jews: *evangelism.* They often view evangelistic campaigns and attempts as specific efforts to convert and destroy the Jewish people. Recall the reflections on evangelism quoted earlier: "If the Christians want to convert the non-Christians in the United States, who does that leave to convert? Just us and the Buddhists." And, "I am concerned that this evangelistic fervor will inevitably result in the children of Jewish converts to Christianity leading in the persecution of my children." Finally, evangelism "promotes a stifling, suppressive climate, intrudes on the privacy of Jews, plans their quick liquidation and extinction, and shelters anti-Semitism."[7]

Evangelism means "sharing or spreading good news." Jewish people connect the term with bad news. In view of these misunderstandings, perhaps good communicators should employ the meaning of the term rather than the term itself. Avoiding the term does not deny that the biblical message must be communicated to all people. In this case, it helps communicate that message more clearly. Certainly, "sharing good news" or "communicating God's message" accurately reflects the biblical teachings on this subject.

Some people may wonder, "Why all this emphasis on terms?" It may even seem insignificant or trivial. The Bible speaks of the believer's responsibility to convey God's truth to men (see, for example, Acts 1:8). To accomplish this, the truth must be accurately communicated, and it is the believer's responsibility to make sure this happens. Ideas are communicated by means of words, but those listening understand words in terms of their own perception and experience. Therefore, for accurate communication of truth, terms must be used that the listeners understand clearly and accurately.

What Not to Do
Communication takes place not only by means of words but by means of actions and attitudes as well. Therefore it is important not to be negative or critical. Do not criticize or convey negative attitudes such as condescension or resentment toward Jewish religious and political leaders or Jewish people in general. The privilege of criticism is an earned one, reserved for family members or friends. Friendship, trust and good will must come first. If they do not, the lines of communication will break.

Another damaging attitude views the Jewish people as a special category or separate class of people apart from others. This often leaves the impression of two opposing groups, "us" and "you" or "them." It may also imply that you consider Jews outsiders. While cultural differences do exist, Jewish people should not be perceived as a group apart or as strange and peculiar, differentiating them from the rest of society. This merely hinders good communication and relationships.

Several actions may inadvertently communicate wrong ideas. Many believers have pictures of Yeshua in their homes and offices. They serve as reminders of him or help produce a spiritual atmosphere. Yet to the Jewish mind this may border on idolatry (Ex 20:4). Imagine you are in your bedroom where you have a picture of Yeshua by your bed. You kneel by your bed to pray as you have your time alone with God. At this point a Jewish person happens to see you. To him it looks like you are bowing and praying to the picture of Yeshua!

Many believers wear a cross as a sign of their devotion or identity as Yeshua's followers. It is a beautiful practice. However, the cross has a different meaning for Jewish people. When Jewish villages were being slaughtered and burned during the Crusades, the Crusades marched behind a flag with the cross on it. When Jewish people were being tortured and killed during the Inquisition, their inquisitors wore the cross as an insignia. When Golda Meir, former prime minister of Israel, had her historic audience with Pope Paul VI in January 1973, the newspapers reported part of their conversation. Mrs. Meir recalled one of her first memories of Christianity, a scene in which a crowd of people stormed through her village, burning it and killing her people. The banner they marched behind was the cross. Events like these have left a deep wound that a cross may re-open. A part of the dialog from Schwarz-Bart's *The Last of the Just* summarizes this so well.

The Christians say they love him, but I think they hate him without knowing it. So they take the cross by the other end and make a sword out of it and strike us with it!

Poor Jesus, if he came back to earth and saw that the pagans had made a sword out of him and used it against his brothers and sisters, he'd be sad, he'd grieve forever.[8]

Yeshua's earliest followers, by the way, used a fish as their symbol, not a cross.

Another essential for good communication involves being aware of what Jewish people despise or desire. A Jewish person does not want to be made a goy ("Gentile"). He usually has no desire to become something different. Most Jews will say, or feel, "I was born a Jew; I'll die a Jew." To most Jews, accepting Yeshua as Messiah means converting, changing their identity and becoming Gentile. It means giving up their Jewish heritage and no longer being Jewish. As previously mentioned, Christianity means persecution and anti-Semitism. It means statements like Luther's "Jews are beasts to be driven out like mad dogs.... Their synagogues ought to be burned."

To many it may mean the ritual and practice of Roman Catholicism. For others it means a religion pagan or polytheistic at its roots. The Jewish perspective sees God as an almighty, invisible being, above and beyond the physical. Many will contrast this with the Christian view of God, as they perceive it, a God-man or man-God. They see this as similar to pagan Greek mythology which had beings which were half god, half man. Further, Jews often think Christians believe in three gods, Father, Son and Holy Spirit, a remnant of polytheism. Jewish people consider these beliefs inferior to their lofty concept of one almighty God. From their understanding, most Jewish people want no part of Christian beliefs. They most certainly have no interest in becoming Gentiles.

The Jew who accepts Yeshua faces the distinct possibility of being considered a *meshumad* ("traitor"). His family and friends would feel he had joined the side of the enemy, a religion that persecuted and killed his people, perhaps even his immediate family. (Recall that Hitler is considered a Christian, as are many others who led in the persecution of Jews.) His family and friends may shun him or cut him off. They may even hold a funeral for him and declare him dead. He would risk all this for what he probably considers just another religion. The Jewish person does not want to be a meshumad.

Neither is he interested in being a sore thumb or oddball, the only Jew who believes in Yeshua. Many think that few Jewish people follow Yeshua. They also feel that if Yeshua were really Messiah, many Jews, including the rabbis, would follow him. They apparently do not, and the average Jewish person refuses to pioneer in this area.

Jewish people desire the same things from life as anyone else: satisfaction, meaning, peace of mind, sense of purpose, life in all its fullness and joy. *L'chaim*, "to life," a familiar Jewish phrase, summarizes these desires. It expresses an important Jewish value, the enjoyment of life, living life to the fullest. Many Jews want to know more about God or to know him more personally. For this reason the more religious spend hours studying Scripture and the commentaries, and exhibit extreme devotion and careful attendance to observances. Widespread Yom Kippur observance also indicates this spiritual hunger and longing to know that things are right between the individual and God. As previously mentioned, "the Jewish nature and soul needs to know God. This is its purpose on earth. Our souls are looking for God and are trying to know God."[9]

Get Things Started Spiritually

A third principle in communicating the message relates to getting things started spiritually. A number of possibilities are available, the first of which involves Jewish symbolism. Home and office decor employing Jewish art or artifacts demonstrates an interest in Jewish people and culture. This can often serve as a conversation starter. Art objects are readily available in a local Jewish bookstore.

Some Gentiles wear a Jewish star (the star of David), the Hebrew word chai, "life," or some other Jewish symbol. When questioned about being Jewish, they will reply in a variety of ways. "I'm Jewish by adoption" refers to Romans 8:15 and 1 Peter 2:10. "I'm a naturalized citizen of the commonwealth of Israel and the Jewish people," refers to Ephesians 2:11-12, 19. "Like a branch grafted into a tree, I view myself as having been grafted into the blessings and heritage of the Jewish people," refers to Romans 11:16-24. All of these replies require a more complete explanation which may start a conversation about spiritual issues. Other replies, with appropriate explanations, are also helpful. "I wear it as a sign of concern and interest in the Jewish people." "I wear it as a sign of appreciation and gratitude to the Jewish people for giving me my faith."

Encouraging discussion about life issues also helps get things started. These issues may include a person's perception or understanding of the world around him, his outlook on life, his view of himself and his purpose on earth, or his feelings about things that concern him. This demonstrates an interest in people and a commitment to communicate at more than surface levels. Such discussions also provide insights into people. If you want to know your Jewish friend better, also ask him how he views his Jewishness, what it means to him, what significance it has and how it relates to his everyday life. If you have any questions about Jewish practice and belief, ask your friend. Use your friendship as an opportunity to learn more about Jewish culture and tradition.

Since Israel interests most Jewish people in some way, the Middle East situation or Israeli news can make for good conversation topics. It allows you an opportunity to show your concern for Israel. You may also get a chance to relate events in Israel to biblical prophecy. Biblical prophecy intrigues many people, but especially Jews because of the close relationship of Jewish people to these prophecies. Some potential areas of interest include the nation Israel in God's prophetic program, prophetic indicators of the "end of days" or predictions about the Messiah.

If at all possible, study the Bible together, looking at what it has to say about these topics. (Appendix A gives outlines for these and other Bible study topics.) Answer questions or objections from Scripture as much as possible from the Tenach (Old Testament). This lends authority to your replies and shows the Jewish nature of your beliefs. Studying the Bible together or in a small group is important because it gives God a chance to communicate directly through the Scriptures. A short series of studies sketching the sweep of God's purpose for the world would provide additional stimulating material for a Bible study.

As you have opportunities, share what God has done in your life and what he is doing now. You may want to tell about the changes God has worked in your life, the void he has filled, or the satisfaction and meaning he has given you. However, since followers of various religious groups make similar claims about their spiritual experience, also talk about God who has acted in history and who gave objective evidence of his existence and actions, for example, through Yeshua's resurrection. You might also relate specifically how God has answered prayer in your life. This demonstrates that God is alive and works in the lives of his people. Offer to pray for your friend's needs.

If you know any Messianic Jews, tell the story of how they came to know God and how he changed their lives. Some of these stories are in print. Even better, introduce your Jewish friends to Messianic Jews or bring them to a Messianic synagogue or fellowship if possible. This visibly demonstrates the consistency between Jewishness and faith in Yeshua.

Attract People to God

The fourth principle for communicating the biblical message involves attracting people to God. Talk about life in all its fullness and about the peace and joy God has provided in difficult situations. Mention atonement for sins, a personal relationship with the God of Abraham, Isaac and Jacob, and a permanent record of your name in the Book of Life. Keep in mind, though, that talking makes little impact unless a lifestyle backs it up. Talk about real life, then vibrantly live it so that others will want it (see Rom 11:11). A Jewish person told a friend, "I keep coming by because you have something real, and I'm searching and wondering if this is it." You want to produce this kind of reaction. In order to attract people to God, it is also important to emphasize certain things. Primarily emphasize that a person does not stop being Jewish when he accepts the Messiah. He does not give up his Jewish heritage, culture and identity. Rather, he gains important Jewish values: atonement as described by Moses, Israel's promised Messiah, and a personal relationship with the God of Abraham, Isaac and Jacob. So he does not give up; he gains. He does not lose his Jewishness; he intensifies it in a biblical way. He becomes a Messianic Jew, a Jewish follower of the Jewish Messiah promised by the Jewish Scriptures. Remember the Jewishness of the biblical faith (see Jn 4:22; Rom 9:4-5; 11:11-27; Acts 26:6-7). The authors of Scripture were Jewish, as were Yeshua and the apostles. And they all, including Paul, retained their Jewishness (Acts 2:46; 3:1; 21:21-26; 22:3; 28:17; 1 Cor 7:18). This does not mean that a Gentile becomes a Jew when he believes in Yeshua, but neither does a Jew stop being Jewish when he accepts the Messiah.

Stress a relationship with the God of Abraham, Isaac and Jacob, not religion. The proper response to God can lead anyone into a relationship with God as personal as Abraham's, and God called him "friend" (Is 41:8). Since God is the source of real life, a personal relationship with him allows man to experience life in its fullness (see Ps 16:11). Mention that many Jewish people have discovered this life through the Messiah. (A survey by Hineni Ministries shows that 15,000-20,000 Jewish people accepted the Messiah in the years 1970-1975 alone.)

As you seek to attract people to God, use and emphasize the Jewish Scriptures. Your Bible is the authority for all you say, and it demonstrates the Jewishness of the message you are sharing. However, a Jewish person may check your Bible to see who published it. If a Jewish press did not publish it, he may reject it. Many Jewish people suspect Bibles published by Christians. They may feel that Christians changed them to suit their interpretations. It is therefore important to have a Bible printed by a Jewish publisher. The Harkavy edition published by the Hebrew Publishing Company,

80 Fifth Avenue, New York, NY 10011, is a good version. Such a Bible is almost exactly like one you already own; it contains all of the books of the Tenach, neither adding nor subtracting anything. The differences are slight: the verse and chapter numbering varies in places, and the order of the prophetic and poetic books (the Prophets and the Writings) differs.

Make Things Clear

The fifth principle of communicating the biblical message focuses on making things clear. It is essential to present clearly God's plan of atonement through the Messiah. A number of useful tools are available to assist you. One of the most effective and popular is the booklet L'chaim, available from An Adventure in Faith, P.O. Box 758, Palm Harbor, FL 33563. This will keep your presentation simple, clear and to the point, and will prevent you from going off on a tangent. It can also give you confidence in what to say next and how to say it. A booklet such as L'chaim serves as an excellent audio-visual aid in communicating the concepts of atonement, because the person you are talking to sees (reads) and hears the message simultaneously. To use a booklet like L'chaim effectively, keep these points in mind:

1. Show your friend the booklet, but keep it in your hands; otherwise he will leaf through the booklet while you are talking and miss what you are saying.

2. Read the booklet aloud, using a pen or pencil to emphasize key points. By reading through the booklet with him, you will keep to the point and will get the maximum benefit of the booklet as an audio-visual aid.

3. Be careful not to add much additional explanation or illustration as you read so you do not go too far afield.

4. If he asks a question, request that he ask it again after you have finished reading through L'chaim. Tell him that he will then see the complete picture and that his question may be answered later in the booklet. *But be sure you respond to his question afterward, if he still has it.*

5. Bring him to a point of decision. Ask him if he would like to accept Yeshua as Messiah. If he says yes, read through the page with the sample prayer and invite him to pray and make his com-

mitment right there or as soon as possible afterward. If he says no, ask him why he feels that way; then try to answer his questions or deal with the objections.

If your friend appears uncertain about accepting Yeshua as Messiah, ask what holds him back and attempt to deal with it. Point out what he has to gain: atonement, a personal relationship with God, a satisfying and meaningful life. At this time you may want to share how God has worked in your life and that he wants to do the same in his life. Challenge him to be honest with God. Urge him to read Isaiah 52:13—53:12 and to reread *L'chaim*. Before reading he should ask God, "If Yeshua is really the Messiah, show me the truth and help me to understand." Make sure you indicate that you would like to talk further about these things. (You could use one of the topics outlined in the appendices.) Then set up a time to get together again.

You can make a transition from a conversation into using *L'chaim* in a number of ways. The keys are imagination and adaptability. Some possible transitions include:

1. "I'd like to share with you some teachings from the Jewish Bible which showed me how to have a personal relationship with God and a satisfying, meaningful life. This booklet summarizes them."

2. "The Jewish Bible contains some important principles on living life to the fullest through a personal relationship with God. This booklet summarizes these teachings. May I share it with you?"

3. "The principles found in this booklet changed my life. They are teachings from the Jewish Bible. I'd like to share them with you."

4. "I'd like to get your reaction to this booklet. It contains some important principles from the Jewish Bible. Would you mind if we went through the booklet together?"

When using such a booklet there is something absolutely vital to keep in mind. Your use of *L'chaim* must grow out of your conversation with your Jewish friend. Simply reading it in a wooden fashion is insufficient. The booklet is a tool to help you communicate the message it contains and which you have personally experienced. Remember, you are not reading a booklet to a telephone pole; you are communicating its contents to a person. Keep it personal.

Is it necessary to use Jewishly oriented material with nonreligious Jewish people? The following example should help illustrate the importance of such literature. At a local college, my wife was conversing with a Jewish girl who was not at all religious. She used the opportunity to talk of Yeshua. Discovering that she had no L'chaim, she decided to use what she had, *The Four Spiritual Laws*. The student listened politely and at the end simply said, "That's nice, but I'm Jewish and it's not relevant to me." About that time a coworker happened by, and my wife asked her for a copy of *L'chaim*. She went through it with the student, and this time the girl followed along with a great deal of interest and openness. She realized the message was for her.

After you have communicated the biblical message and your friend has committed his life to Yeshua, following through is very important. Carefully go through the pages following the sample prayer in *L'chaim*. This will briefly acquaint your friend with the principles of assurance and growth in the spiritual life. Give him a modern language Bible or B'rit Hadasha as soon as possible and urge him to begin reading the gospels of Mark and Matthew. It is important to set up a time, within forty-eight hours if possible, to get together again so you can share some principles which helped you grow in your relationship with God. This will help to solidify his commitment and aid him in his spiritual growth. With this appointment start a series of studies—preferably once a week—on the basic principles of the spiritual life, such as growth and the role of the Holy Spirit, and on some of the objections and questions that his family and friends may raise about his faith. *Relating to God*, available through An Adventure in Faith, is an excellent study guide dealing with these issues. If a local Messianic congregation or fellowship is available, urge him to participate in it. Sometimes a home Bible study group is a workable alternative, especially if other Jewish believers are involved; it is certainly a good idea before a visit to a church. The presence and encouragement of other Messianic Jews is especially vital in the early stages of his spiritual life. Offer to take your friend to such gatherings. This will ensure that he knows at least one other person and will also give you the opportunity to have an enjoyable time.

Unbridled enthusiasm on the part of new followers of Yeshua has frequently led to unnecessary family tension. Encourage your friend to act with great discretion and tact. Imagine you are a parent whose child has returned from college during a vacation. As a strong evangelical you have diligently brought up your child to respect and adhere to an evangelical faith. When your child returns home this time, he tells you excitedly about a new discovery he has made: "Mom, Dad, I've found out what life's all about! All these years we've been wrong. Baha'i is God's real revelation and the only true religion!" The feelings you would experience would not begin to be as strong as those of many Jewish parents whose children return home as followers of Yeshua. Out of respect for his family, the new Messianic Jew should not display pictures of Yeshua, crosses or tracts. If he displays anything, it should be the Jewish Bible. He needs to show by his changed life that God has made him a better family member. He should earn the right to share the Messiah with his family and friends. Alert your friend, also, not to criticize Judaism or his parents' beliefs and practices. If they go to synagogue services, he should attend with them. He must demonstrate that he has become a better Jewish person. Then he will get the opportunity to relate how he discovered meaning and satisfaction in life and a relationship with God through biblical or Messianic Judaism and through the Jewish Messiah. He should answer questions and share Yeshua gently and tactfully and not shove his new faith down their throats. When he relates these things, he should use the Jewish Bible, especially Isaiah 53, and *L'chaim*.

Alert him not to expect things to be perfect. He will still face problems, but he can now turn these problems over to God and trust him to bring him through with a supernatural peace (1 Pet 5:7; Phil 4:6-7). Tell him that God wants to hear from him about everything (Phil 4:6-7). Remind him, though, that God will answer his prayers in any one of four different ways: yes, no, wait, and I've got something better for you. Assure him that God will always do what is best for him (Rom 8:28), even if he does not understand what God is doing. In all things, remember that the Spirit of God (*Ruach HaKodesh* in Hebrew) will show him what is right and what is wrong. It's his job, not yours.

For more information on communicating the biblical message to Jewish people, write the International Hebrew Christian Alliance, P.O. Box 758, Palm Harbor, FL 33563.

APPENDICES

APPENDIX A:
USING THE JEWISH BIBLE

After his resurrection Yeshua spent a lot of time instructing his disciples, showing them how the Jewish Scriptures spoke about him. This survey of Scripture may have included perspectives similar to those found in chapter two, "The Jewish People in the Program of God." Yeshua demonstrated how the Tenach was integrally tied to his person. One memorable occasion of such instruction occurred during a walk to the city of Emmaus (Lk 24:25-28), at which time he patiently showed what Jewish Scripture, from beginning to end, had to say about the Messiah.

This chapter is intended to recapture Yeshua's methodology. The following approaches are designed so that you can logically guide your Jewish friend, using his own Bible, to a consideration of atonement through the Messiah.

It is important that you use a Jewish translation of the Bible. In this way your Jewish friend can see the issues from his own Bible. Remember, often he won't accept Bibles published by non-Jewish publishers. The discussions in the approaches suggested here are built around the text of the Harkavy edition of the Holy Scriptures, published by the Hebrew Publishing Company, 80 Fifth Avenue, New York, NY 10011.

Learn the outlines of the approaches. It is easier to do this if you group your learning and thinking by verses and concepts. If you take the time and trouble to learn these approaches, you will have many times of effective communication with Jewish people. You may want to put the outlines on a slip of paper in front of your Bible as a memory guide. However, do not write in your Jewish Bible. Some Jewish people would be deeply offended at this.

Each of the approaches is designed to be used with a specific type of Jewish person or to meet a specific need or question.

The "Real Life" approach is an expansion of L'chaim and demonstrates from the Jewish Bible the principles of experiencing real life as God intended. This serves as a good review of L'chaim (or substitutes for it if you have time in the initial conversation) and shows the Jewish person the plan of atonement from his own Bible. This is a general approach, usable with any Jewish person who is willing to read what his Scriptures teach.

The "Principles of Atonement" approach is a detailed study of atonement from the Jewish Bible. It is especially effective with the Orthodox Jew or the Jewish person who considers the Hebrew Scriptures as authoritative or instructive. It can be used whenever a Jewish person is interested in the teachings of the Jewish Bible about atonement for sins. You can use it very profitably near the time of Yom Kippur (Day of Atonement).

The "Messianic Prophecy" approach details the predictions of the Jewish prophets about the nature and identity of the Messiah. It is effective with any Jewish person who wants to know who Messiah is or what the Jewish Scriptures say about the Messiah. Usually the Orthodox or Conservative Jew will be more interested in Messiah and his coming.

The "National Prophecy" approach outlines God's dealing with Israel past, present and future, especially in relation to fulfilled prophecy. This is a good approach to use with a person interested in Israel but not in God, religion or Jewishness. It is an excellent tool to awaken interest in God and the Bible and to establish respect for biblical teachings. It can serve as an effective transition to a discussion of atonement through the Messiah.

The "End-Time Prophecy" approach outlines the predictions of both the prophets and Yeshua about the events taking place prior to his return. It can be used in much the same way as the "National Prophecy" approach and also to validate Yeshua's claims to Messiahship and deity. Although many Jewish people have accepted Yeshua as a result of this kind of approach, some people may feel uncomfortable with this particular perspective on prophecy. If this is the case for you, another of the approaches mentioned in the Appendix will be more suitable.

The "Relationship with God" approach deals with man's problem in trying to be right before God by obeying God's laws or living a good life. It outlines what God expects, the impossibility of meeting his requirements, the necessity of a "new heart," and the principles God follows (grace and atonement by sacrifice) in giving man a new heart. The covenants he has made, and especially the new covenant, show God's grace and the necessity of sacrifice. This is an excellent approach for those who feel that living properly before God will earn a relationship with him.

The apostles commonly used the "Resurrection" approach as their reason for believing the biblical message (see Acts 2:24-36). It provides the clearest objective evidence for the truth of Yeshua's Messiahship and deity. It is exceptionally good for those who would like to have evidence or reasons for the validity of the biblical message. Three thousand Jews responded to its proclamation when it was first presented.

When using these approaches, locate the particular passage in the Jewish Bible. (Note: Verses in the Jewish Bible are sometimes numbered differently from those in Christian versions. If for some reason you are not using a Jewish Bible, be sure to find these texts and note their verse numbers before giving any of these presentations.) Then ask your Jewish friend to read aloud the verses involved before you ask the questions about the verses or make the explanations. Point to what you are explaining or asking questions about. In this way your Jewish friend reads for himself what his own Bible teaches. The questions you ask and the explanations you give are in regular type. The desired answers are in italics.

If your friend does not give you the proper answer, guide him into seeing and giving the correct response.

How to Present the Principles of Experiencing Real Life
A. *Introduction.*
1. L'chaim is a familiar phrase among Jewish people and expresses an important Jewish concept: the enjoyment of life, living life to the fullest.
2. Life! But what's it all about?
3. Some people feel that a satisfying, worthwhile life consists of a good education, close friends, a good marriage and healthy children, success in a business or profession, helping those in need, involvement with Israel and the Jewish community, or a good time.
4. These are important. But is that all there is to life? Is that really all?
5. We all know people who live like this but who aren't satisfied, who still feel an emptiness deep inside. Then something must be missing.
6. There is more to life.
7. The Jewish Bible gives us the clues to enjoyment and meaning in life today.
B. *One of the first things the Jewish Bible points out is that real life–life with all its meaning and enjoyment–has its source in God.*
1. Psalm 16:11 describes the path of life.
a. How is the satisfying, worthwhile life described? *Fullness of joy, pleasures for evermore.* That certainly sounds like a desirable lifestyle to have.
b. Who is the source of this kind of Life? *God (Thou).*
c. What phrases indicate that a close, personal relationship with God is necessary for this life? *In thy presence, at thy right hand.*
2. Isaiah 41:8 shows how intimate this personal relationship with God can be. What does God call Abraham in the last part of the verse? *My friend.* Now that's a close relationship with God!
3. You know, deep down, just about everyone wants a life and relationship like this.
a. A Jewish scientist put it this way: "The Jewish nature and soul needs to know God. This is its purpose on earth. Our souls are looking for God and are trying to know God."

b. But if they want it, why aren't people experiencing this life and relationship?

C. *People do not enjoy real life because man has separated himself from God.*

1. Leviticus 19:2b (begin reading with "Ye shall be holy... ").

a. What is the standard by which man is to live? *God's holiness.* In other words, God's perfect character.

b. Any deviation from God's character, any violation of his standard, is called sin.

2. Obviously, then, all of us have sinned.

a. Ecclesiastes 7:20. How many people are there on the earth that do not sin? *Not one!*

b. Psalm 53:3-4. From God's viewpoint, how many people are meeting his standards? *Not one!*

3. Habakkuk 1:13a (read up to "iniquity").

a. What can't God allow in his presence? *Evil, iniquity.*

b. Why? *Because of his purity (his holiness and righteousness).* You may want to compare Psalm 5:5-7 and Numbers 14:18.

4. Because sin is a violation of his standard and character, God must judge man's sin and reject it if he is to be a just God (see Nahum 1:3).

a. Jeremiah 31:29a (read up to "iniquity"). What does sin result in? *Death.* This is a reference not merely to physical death but to spiritual death, the total absence of any relationship or connection with God.

b. Ezekiel 18:20a (read up to "die"). Who will suffer this spiritual death? *The soul (person) who sins.* According to what we've read before, that includes all of us. See Psalm 9:18.

c. This condition we're in because of our sins is described in another way in Isaiah 59:2. What does sin cause? *A separation between us and God.*

5. But can't man solve the problem by living properly, by prayer, repentance and good deeds?

D. *No, the Jewish Bible shows us that man cannot remove the sin barrier by his own efforts.*

1. Psalm 143:2. Who can make himself acceptable to God? *No man living.*

2. Isaiah 64:5 (read up to "garment"). How does God view our best efforts, our good deeds, our righteousnesses? *As a filthy garment, as unclean.* See Ezekiel 33:12-13.

3. Psalm 49:8-9.

a. *Redeem,* in this context, refers to setting someone free from the problem of the sin barrier.

b. Who can free himself or anyone else from the sin barrier (v. 8)? *No one.*

c. Why can't this be done (v. 9)? *Their redemption is too precious. (It costs too much.)*

4. Therefore, the Jewish Bible teaches that man cannot do enough to solve the problem of spiritual death and separation from God.

5. Psalm 49:16. Who must then take the initiative and provide the solution to this problem? *God.*

6. Psalm 51:3. What is God's solution for the sin barrier based on? *His loving-kindness and mercy.* See Psalm 86:13; 25:7, 11; Isaiah 43:25.

7. God's provision is described in the Jewish Bible.

E. *The sin barrier can be removed by believing God's Word (faith) and by having the blood of the atonement.*

1. Genesis 15:6. Abraham was an example of how the sin barrier can be removed.

a. What did Abraham do? *Believed God.*

b. What was the result? *God counted it as righteousness.* In other words, God accepted him.

2. Isaiah 26:3-4. We need to follow the same pattern.

a. "Perfect peace" is the result of being in harmony with God.

b. Why does God give man this perfect peace (v. 3)? *Because he trusts in God.* Trust is a synonym for faith.

c. How long should we trust God (v. 4)? *Forever.*

3. Moses said that one more thing is essential.

a. Leviticus 17:11. What is necessary if we are to have atonement? *Blood (or a sacrifice).*

b. Leviticus 10:17. Why had God given the procedure of the sin offering? *To bear the iniquity of the people and make atonement for them.*

c. Leviticus 4:35 (begin reading with "and the priest"). What is the result of offering the sacrifice? *Atonement and forgiveness of sin.*

d. The Hebrew word for atonement (kipper) means to ransom by means of a substitute, to turn away divine wrath by an appropriate offering and thus accomplish a reconciliation between God and man. So a life had to be given up (in this case the life of the sacrifice) for the sin barrier to be removed.

4. But why would God want to go through the awful procedure of killing an animal? *When the offerer saw the sacrifice suffering and bleeding for the sins which he had committed, he was impressed with the awfulness of sin and the penalty of death the sinner deserved.* (On death as punishment for sin, see Ezekiel 18:4, 20.) The sacrifice showed him three characteristics of God:

a. He is holy—because he hates evil.

b. He is just—because he does not leave sin unpunished.

c. He is merciful—because he is ready to pardon the truly repentant and believing person by providing a substitute for him.

5. The animal sacrifices thus provided the blood of atonement and were an act of faith acceptable to God. So both faith and the sacrifices were necessary to remove the sin barrier.

6. But without a priesthood and without a temple, there can be no sacrifices (Lev 1:5). So how can we have the blood of atonement today?

F. *God has provided the blood of atonement for today.*

1. Isaiah 53:5-6, 8, 10, 12.

a. For what was he wounded and bruised (v. 5)? *Our transgressions and iniquities.*

b. Chastisement means punishment (v. 5), so our punishment was put on him.

c. What did the Lord do (v. 6)? *Caused the iniquity of all of us to fall on him.*

d. Why did he die (v. 8)? *For the transgressions of the people.* The Hebrew word for "recompense for guilt" is asham, the term which also means "trespass offering" (Lev 5). Therefore, he dies as a sacrifice for sin, to provide the blood of atonement (Is 53:10).

e. As a result of his death, what did he take off (v. 12)? *The sin of many.*

f. If he has died, how can his days be prolonged (v. 10)? *He must come back to life!*

2. The prologue to this chapter (Is 52:13-15) gives some indication as to the identity of the "he" of this passage.

a. He is described as God's servant, who will be exalted.

b. Elsewhere, Isaiah equates this servant of God with Messiah. See, for example, Isaiah 42:1; 49:6.

3. God's provision of the blood of atonement through the Messiah follows the same principles which God set up in the sacrifice system.

a. The sin offering provided atonement for a man by means of a sacrifice (Lev 1:3-5).

b. During Pesach (Passover), atonement was made for a family by means of a sacrifice (Ex 12).

c. During Yom Kippur (Day of Atonement), atonement was made for the nation by means of a sacrifice (Lev 16).

d. Messiah provided atonement for everyone by means of his sacrifice (Is 53).

4. As we've seen, under the sacrifice system personal faith was necessary along with the blood of atonement. So faith is also necessary with the sacrifice of Messiah. He should be the object of our faith today.

5. But how can we know who Messiah is?

G. *God made sure we could recognize Messiah by certain specific identifying marks. These are described by the prophets of Israel.*

1. His ancestry was to be from the family of David (Jer 23:5-6).

2. The city of his birth was to be Bethlehem (Mic 5:1).

3. He was to have a supernatural nature (Jer 23:5-6; Mic 5:1; Is 9:5-6).

4. The purpose of his coming was to restore man's relationship with God (Is 49:6).

5. He was to die (Is 53:8; Dan 9:26).

6. The manner of his execution was to be crucifixion (Ps 22:14-17).

7. He was to rise from the dead (Is 53:10; Ps 16:10).

8. The time of his coming was to be before the destruction of the Second Temple in 70 CE (Dan 9:26).[1]

9. Do you have any idea if anyone has fulfilled these prophecies, or has even come close?

a. History tells us that Yeshua fulfilled these and many other prophecies.

b. There are at least forty-eight specific prophecies concerning

Messiah that Yeshua fulfilled. The probability that one person could fulfill all of these is very remote (Peter Stoner in *Science Speaks* [Evanston, Ill.: Moody Press, 1969] estimates the probability at 1 out of 10^{157}).

c. During his lifetime many people called him Messiah ("Christ" is the Greek translation of Messiah) and believed in him (Mt 16:16; Jn 1:45-51; Acts 6:7).

d. Many people since that time, both Jews and Gentiles, have had their sins forgiven and have begun a personal relationship with the God of Abraham, Isaac and Jacob through Messiah Yeshua. Through him one becomes a completed person; that is, a Jewish person becomes a completed Jew.

10. Since the blood of atonement has been provided through Yeshua the Messiah, there is only one thing left for you to do. (Go over point 5 of *L'chaim.*)

How to Present the Principles of Atonement
A. *Introduction.*
1. A prominent Jewish scientist and speaker said recently, "The Jewish nature and soul needs to know God. Our souls are looking for God and are trying to know God."
2. He was stressing the importance of having a proper relationship with God.
3. The Jewish Bible explains how we can have a proper relationship with God. Read Psalm 11:7.
a. What is God called? *Righteous.*
b. What pleases God? *Righteousness.*
c. The last phrase in the verse can be translated, "The upright will behold his countenance."
d. Righteousness means rightness, a right standing before God, a state of being upright and pure in God's sight, a clean unhindered relationship with God.
e. God is deeply concerned about our being righteous, or he wouldn't have stressed it so much here.
B. *Therefore, it's important to know how a person can achieve righteousness or a right standing before God.*
1. What three things have the rabbis taught us are necessary in order to be righteous?

a. Prayer, repentance and mitzvot (good deeds).

b. These are good in their proper place; but there is a deeper problem.

2. Isaiah 64:5 describes this problem.

a. How does God view us? Unclean.

b. What is God's evaluation of our good deeds, our religious works, our good living? Filthy rags.

c. If this is what God thinks of the best we can produce, then we're in real trouble before God unless there is some other way to become righteous (see Ezek 33:12-13).

3. Genesis 15:6. Abraham achieved righteousness before God. Maybe his life can give us a clue as to how we can do the same.

a. What did Abraham do? Believed in the Lord.

b. What was the result? God counted it as righteousness.

c. So Abraham got right with God because of his faith.

4. Habakkuk 2:4-6. If God required faith from Abraham for righteousness, he probably also requires faith on our parts.

a. The word just is a synonym for righteous.

b. How or why does a righteous man live? By or because of his faith.

c. Isaiah 26:3-4. The word trust is a synonym for faith.

(1) Why does God keep a person in perfect peace? Because of his faith.

(2) Perfect peace indicates a settled, harmonious relationship with God.

(3) How long should we trust in God? Forever. God wants us to continue believing in him.

(4) The Talmud underscores this: "Rabbi Salmai gave the following exposition: 613 commandments were given to Moses. . . . Then came the prophet Habakkuk and reduced all the commands to one, as it is written [Hab 2:4], 'The just shall live by his faith' " (Makkot 23-24).

d. Faith is vital; but you could have faith that if you plant stones in the ground, you'll get petrified trees. It doesn't do much good to have faith if it's placed in the wrong thing. We have to find out what God wants us to place our faith in today to be made righteous.

C. Psalm 49:8-9, 16. The issue that's involved in being made righteous is atonement for sins or the redemption of the soul.

1. Who can provide the means by which to redeem his or another's soul (v. 8)? *No one.*

2. The word *redeem* here means giving something as a ransom in exchange for freeing the soul from the penalty and power of sin and death.

3. Why can't anyone pay the ransom price for the human soul (v. 9)? *It costs too much.*

4. How then can the redemption of the soul or atonement for sins be accomplished (v. 16)? *God must do it.*

D. *How God redeems the soul and provides atonement for sin.*

1. Exodus 12:21-24. God's way is demonstrated by Pesach (Passover).

a. Each family was commanded to kill the Passover lamb and put blood on the doorposts of their home.

b. What would happen when God saw the blood on the door? *He would protect the family from the destroyer.*

c. In other words, if a lamb was killed, the family members wouldn't be killed or harmed. In essence the lamb gave up its life for the sake of the family.

d. How long was this procedure to be observed? *Forever.*

2. Leviticus 16:15-16, 30, 34. God's way of redemption and atonement is also demonstrated by Yom Kippur (Day of Atonement).

a. The priest had to sacrifice the goat as a sin offering on behalf of the people (v. 15).

b. Why did atonement have to be made (v. 16)? *Because of uncleanness, the sins and transgressions of the people.*

c. What does atonement mean? *Pardon for our sins.* The Hebrew term for atonement (*kipper*) means to ransom by means of a substitute. God's just punishment for sin was averted by an appropriate sacrifice. This accomplished a reconciliation between God and man.

d. What was the result of the Day of Atonement sacrifice (v. 30)? *People were clean from their sins before God.*

e. A goat was killed for the people so they could receive atonement or forgiveness of sins from God. Ezekiel 18:4, 20 says that the person who sins must die. Therefore, the goat died in place of the people.

f. How long was this procedure to be continued (v. 34)? *Forever.*

3. God's way of atonement and redemption can also be seen in the sin offering.

a. Leviticus 1:3-5. When the offerer brought his sacrifice, he placed his hands on the head of the animal (a symbol of identification) and confessed his sins. His sins then became identified with the animal and thus necessitated the death of the animal (see Ezek 18:4, 20). The animal gave up its life for the offerer.

b. Leviticus 10:17. Why had God given the sin offering? *To bear the iniquity of the people and make atonement for them.* The sins of the people were taken away or carried by the sin offering.

c. Leviticus 4:35. What happened when the sacrifice had been killed and atonement had been made? *Sin was forgiven.*

d. Therefore, for sin to be forgiven and for atonement to be made, the animal had to be sacrificed.

e. You might ask, "Why was the sacrifice of an innocent animal necessary?"

4. Atonement and redemption are based on the exchange-of-life principle.

a. Remember:

(1) Pesach: a lamb died so the family wouldn't die at the hands of the destroyer.

(2) Yom Kippur: a goat bore the sins of the people and was sacrificed to atone for sins.

(3) Sin offering: an animal was sacrificed to atone for a man's sins, so he could be forgiven.

(4) Ezekiel 18:4, 20 reminds us that the punishment for sin is death.

b. Leviticus 17:11.

(1) What is necessary to make atonement for sins? *Blood.*

(2) What does the blood stand for? *Life,* the innocent life (the sacrifice) dying for the guilty life (the offerer).

(3) Therefore, an exchange of life is necessary to provide forgiveness of sins and a clean relationship with God.

(4) The Talmud verifies this. "Does not atonement come through the blood, as it is said: For it is the blood that maketh atonement by reason of the life?" (Yoma 5a).

c. Leviticus 1:3-5. The procedure of the sacrifice.

(1) In addition to providing atonement, the sacrifice procedure

served as a picture story or object lesson to convey spiritual realities. Participation in this procedure was calculated to impress the offerer with the awfulness of sins and the penalty of death that the sinner deserved (Ezek 18:4). It also showed him the holiness, justice and mercy of God—holiness because God hates all evil, justice because he doesn't leave sin unpunished, and mercy because he is ready to pardon the truly repentant and believing person by providing a substitute for him.

(2) When the offerer brought his animal sacrifice, he placed his hands on the head of the animal (a symbol of identification) and acknowledged his sins. His sins then became identified with the animal.

(3) The action can be viewed as the animal giving up its life for the offerer so that the offerer could continue living. The offerer gives his sins to the animal, so the animal must die (Ezek 18:4). In exchange the offerer gets the innocent life of the animal and continues to live. There was, therefore, an exchange of life.[2]

(4) It is true that repentance and faith were necessary. The sacrifice had to be accompanied by repentance and faith. Psalm 51:19, 21 affirms that both aspects were essential. The offerer had to turn from his sin and trust God to forgive his sin on the basis of the exchange-of-life principle illustrated by the sacrifice. But repentance apart from the sacrifice was insufficient because blood was required for atonement (Lev 17:11).

5. Many people like to set aside sacrifice as the means of atonement, saying it is unnecessary. This is incorrect.

a. 1 Samuel 3:14. What is the way in which sin is purged or atoned for? *Sacrifice and offering.*

b. The importance of the sacrifice system has been consistently recognized by the ancient rabbis, as indicated by this passage from the Jerusalem Talmud. "They asked Wisdom, 'What is the punishment of the sinner?' Wisdom answered, 'Evil pursues sinners' [Prov 13:21]. They asked Prophecy, 'What is the punishment of the sinner?' Prophecy answered, 'The soul that sinneth it shall die' [Ezek 18:4]. They asked the Torah, 'What is the punishment of the sinner?' Torah answered, 'Let him bring a guilt offering and it shall be forgiven unto him, as it is said, "and it shall be accepted for him to make atonement for him" ' [Lev 1:4]."[3]

6. Leviticus 1:5. But God also had some other requirements concerning the sacrifice.

a. Who was supposed to sprinkle the blood of the sacrifice? *Aaron's sons.*

b. Where was it supposed to be sprinkled? *By the door of the Tabernacle.* Later the Temple replaced the Tabernacle.

c. What happened to the Temple and the Temple records in 70 CE? *They were destroyed by Titus and the Roman legions.* The Temple records included genealogies or "family trees."

d. Then can we be absolutely sure who the sons of Aaron are today? *Not without the records.*

e. In addition, since the Temple is not in existence, we're not meeting either of God's two requirements for the sacrifice and atonement: Aaron's sons officiating and sacrifices made at the Temple.

f. That means you and I don't have atonement for our sins; they remain unforgiven, unless God has provided the blood atonement in another way.

E. *How God provides the blood of atonement today.*

1. Daniel 9:24-26.

a. This is a complicated prophecy, but several things are clear about it.

b. What is the purpose of the seventy weeks? *To make an end of sins, make reconciliation for iniquity, bring in everlasting righteousness.* In other words, it has to do with atonement and forgiveness of sins and producing righteousness.

c. Who is the person whose coming is predicted (v. 25)? *The anointed, the prince. Anointed* is the same Hebrew term as *Messiah.* So the prophecy concerns the mission of Messiah the prince.

d. What will happen to Messiah, the anointed, after threescore and two weeks (v. 26)? *He'll be cut off.* This is a descriptive way of saying Messiah will be killed!

e. So the prophecy has something to do with atonement for sins and the coming and death of Messiah, and these two aspects are connected in some way. There is a more complete picture of this in Isaiah.

2. Isaiah 52:13—53:12.

a. 52:13—53:3.

(1) Is this passage talking about a person, a nation or what (v. 13)? *A person.* The personal pronouns show this.

(2) Is he a lowly or exalted person? *Exalted.*

(3) What's going to happen to his visage or appearance (v. 14)? *It will be marred more than any man.* Apparently, he will go through severe physical beating.

(4) How did the people react to him (v. 3)? *Despised and rejected him.*

b. 53:4-12.

(1) Whose sorrows and griefs is he bearing, his or ours (v. 4)? *Ours.* And what is our estimation of these happenings? *He is being stricken by God.* In other words, he is suffering for us, and we're saying God is punishing him.

(2) Why was he wounded and bruised (v. 5)? *Because of our iniquities and transgressions* (i.e., sins). The Hebrew word for "wounded" *(chalal)* literally means "pierced."

(3) What did God cause to fall on him (v. 6)? *Our iniquities.*

(4) What do the terms *lamb* and *sheep* remind you of (v. 7)? *The sacrifice animals.*

(5) Why was he killed ("cut off out of the land of the living") (v. 8)? *Because of our transgressions.*

(6) Because of his death, what did he take off (v. 12)? *The sin of many.*

(7) If he has died, how can his days be prolonged (v. 10)? *He is not left dead. He is raised from the dead* (see also Ps 16:10).

c. Who is this person who is to die as an atonement for sins?

(1) How is he described in 52:13? *God's servant who will be exalted and very high.*

(2) This is obviously a description of Messiah, who is God's servant and who will be exalted (see Is 42:1).

d. It's true that many of our religious leaders say this passage is talking about the nation Israel, but the passage doesn't indicate this.

(1) As we saw earlier, on the surface the passage appears to be describing an individual, who in 52:13-15 is described in terms used for Messiah.

(2) If the passage is talking about Israel, who is "my people" in v. 8? This is the usual reference to Israel.

(3) In v. 9 can Israel be honestly described as "having done no violence," "having no deceit in his mouth"? *No.* Isaiah said earlier

(29:13) that Israel dishonored God with their mouths and claimed a relationship with God that they didn't have.

(4) In v. 10 the word for "recompense for guilt" is *asham* or "trespass offering." The trespass offering in Leviticus 5 had to be perfect, without spot and without blemish. Can you say that Israel is without spot or blemish, perfect? Can they fit the qualifications of a trespass offering? *Of course not* (compare Is 65:1-7).

(5) The evidence from the passage itself indicates that an individual, the Messiah, is the subject of the prophecy. Early Jewish scholarship bears this out.

(6) As Raphael Loewe has noted: "Surviving Jewish exegesis up to the end of the Amoraic period (500 CE) suggests that it was then frequently, perhaps even generally, assumed without question that the figure referred to was the Messiah."[4]

3. You might ask "How can Messiah's sacrifice be adequate to atone for the sins of all men? How can one sacrifice take the place of the many and continual sacrifices prescribed by Moses?" The answer is found in the uniqueness of Messiah's nature.

a. Micah 5:1 (read through "ruler in Israel").

(1) What kind of person does this refer to? *One who will rule Israel.* This is a designation of the Messiah.

(2) Read the rest of the verse. How is he described in this next phrase? *From everlasting.*

(3) Can anyone other than God be described as from everlasting? *No.* (See Ps 90:2; 41:14 if necessary.)

b. Isaiah 9:5-6 (read through "upon his shoulder").

(1) Is this talking about a person? *Yes.*

(2) Whom do these phrases describe (v. 6)? *Messiah the King.*

(3) What are his titles (v. 5)? *Wonderful, counselor of the mighty God, etc.*

(4) Can just anyone act as God's counselor? *No.* (See Is 40:13 if necessary.)

c. The Messiah, as the complete revelation of God in human form, volunteers to be our substitute (see Heb 1:1-3; 10:1-10). He is the full radiance of God's glory, the flawless manifestation of his reality. So it is partially that God himself becomes our substitute. He is hurt by sin and suffers to be able to forgive us. He takes our punishment on himself in the person of the Messiah to relieve us of

guilt and judgment. The animal sacrifices pointed to this. This forgiveness is very costly to God and shows his love. The verification and vindication of the whole process is the resurrection of Messiah.[5]
d. It is because of this uniqueness of his nature that Messiah could be the one sacrifice to atone for the sins of all men.
F. *God has not changed the exchange-of-life principle of atonement.*[6]
1. The only difference is that Messiah took the place of the animal sacrifice. (Read 2 Cor 5:21; Is 53:4-6.)
2. Because our lives are sinful, we deserve to die. The Messiah is now the one who, when we identify with him, is considered to have died for each of us personally.
3. In return, the Messiah gives over his life to the believer in him. In a sense, the believer lives on now with the pure life of the Messiah and therefore has a proper and personal relationship with God.
4. The believer thus has his name written permanently in the Book of Life, receives eternal life, life that will last forever, and will ultimately be in the presence of God.
5. In addition, the kind of life the believer receives is a life of power to enable him to deal with problems. This is possible because of Messiah's quality of life. Apart from his life in us, we can fall prey to the weaknesses of our own nature which thwart us.
G. *How then can you personally appropriate the atonement through the Messiah? These several passages summarize how. (Read L'chaim, beginning with point 5.)*

How to Present Messianic Prophecy
A. *A rabbi said recently: "Time is rushing on; God must take a hand in history as he did in the time of Moses. This is the time when Messiah will come; he might even come tomorrow." If the Messiah were to appear today, how would we be able to recognize him?*
1. The Hebrew Scriptures tell us how to recognize Israel's Messiah. Here we find Messiah's credentials.
2. His place of birth is specified in Micah 5:1 (read through "ruler in Israel").
a. What kind of person is being described? *A ruler for God in*

Israel. This is a designation of Messiah's function.

b. Where was he to be born or "come forth" from? *Bethlehem.*

3. The manner of his birth is described in Isaiah 7.

a. Isaiah is standing before Ahaz and makes his statements with Ahaz and his household (the house of David) standing around (vv. 10-17). He tells Ahaz to ask God for a sign. Ahaz refuses. Isaiah then replies, "Nevertheless; house of David [this goes beyond Ahaz], God will give you a sign." He uses the plural consistently in describing God's sign to the house (dynasty, line) of David. In verse 16 he returns to the singular and the specific message to Ahaz.

b. What would the Lord give (v. 14)? *A sign.* The Hebrew word for sign is usually used to mean miracle (Gen 9:13-15; Num 14:22; Deut 11:3; 29:2). So there is something unusual about the way Messiah is born.

c. What is the sign? *A young woman would give birth to a son.* The Hebrew word for young woman is *almah,* which is consistently used in the Jewish Bible for a young woman who is a virgin. It is also rendered this way by the Septuagint, earliest of translations (approximately 200 BCE).

d. It wouldn't be a miracle or sign for a young married woman to have a child because that happens all the time. But it would be a miraculous sign for a virgin to have a child!

e. What name is given to this child? *Immanuel.* That means "God with us." So this child, the Messiah, is "God with us."

f. Let's go back to Micah 5:1. The Messiah is to be born in Bethlehem and rule Israel. But look at the rest of the passage.

(1) How is Messiah described? *His goings forth are from of old, from everlasting.* Literally, Micah is saying that "his existence has been from of old, from the days of eternity."

(2) This is certainly a miraculous sign. He is human in his birth at Bethlehem, but he has existed from eternity. He is born as a human being, yet he is also "God with us"!

4. The time of his coming is predicted in Daniel 9:25-26.

a. After a certain specified period of time, who will appear (v. 25)? *The anointed, the prince.* "The anointed" is the literal translation of the term *Messiah.*

b. What happens after the Messiah is cut off or killed (v. 26)? *The city (Jerusalem) and sanctuary (Temple) are destroyed.* From the context of this passage it's easy to see that Daniel is talking about the Second Temple (later beautified by Herod).

c. The prophecy says that the Second Temple will be destroyed after the Messiah comes. When was it destroyed? *In 70 CE. So Messiah had to come before then.*

5. His reception is described in Isaiah 53:1-3.

a. Is the prophet talking about a man, a nation, or what? *A man.*

b. How is he treated by the people (v. 3)? *Despised, rejected.*

c. Look at Isaiah 52:13-15. These verses form the introduction to chapter 53. The person mentioned is described as God's servant, who in the future will be exalted and very high. This is a description of Messiah (compare Is 42:1). Isaiah 53:1-3 says he will be rejected by the people!

6. His unique nature is pictured in Isaiah 9:5-6 (read through "upon his shoulder").

a. Who is this talking about? *A child, a son.*

b. Whom would these phrases (v. 6) describe? *Messiah the King.*

c. What are his titles (v. 5)? *Wonderful, counselor of the mighty God, of the Everlasting Father, Prince of Peace.*

d. Can just anyone act as God's counselor? *No.* (Compare Is 40:13 if necessary.)

e. These titles express the uniqueness of Messiah's nature; there is something supernatural about him.

f. Compare this with what we read in Isaiah 7:14 and Micah 5:1.

(1) Messiah is described as existing from eternity.

(2) He is "God with us."

7. The death of Messiah is also mentioned by the prophets.

a. Daniel 9:26.

(1) Remember, *anointed* means Messiah.

(2) What will happen to Messiah after "threescore and two weeks?" *He will be cut off,* that is, killed.

b. The manner of his death is described in Psalm 22:15-17.

(1) This has consistently been recognized as a Messianic psalm.[7] David wrote it in 1000 BCE, at a time when stoning was the method of capital punishment. So David was describing a manner of death which was foreign to the people of his day. Let's look at his description.

(2) What happened to Messiah's bones (v. 15)? *They are out of joint.*

(3) What happened to the water content of Messiah's body (v. 16)? *Dried up, dehydrated.*

(4) The words "they threaten" (v. 17) are in italics, an editorial indication that this is an interpolation and the words aren't found in the Hebrew text.

(a) This can also be translated "they pierced my hands and my feet." There are manuscripts to support both readings.

(b) Whatever the translation, the main point is that the hands and feet are seriously injured.

(c) The rest of the psalm pictures an execution scene in which people are standing around mocking while an individual is suffering and dying and is naked in the process.

(5) Describe crucifixion as done by the Romans, showing how all these descriptions fit death by crucifixion.

(6) Crucifixion was not used as a means of execution until the time of the Romans, about 200 BCE, eight hundred years after the writing of this psalm.

(7) Crucifixion is the only known form of execution which pierces or otherwise injures the hands and feet. David predicted that this is the way Messiah's death would come about.

8. The purpose of his death is detailed in Daniel and Isaiah.

a. Daniel 9:24-26.

(1) We've already noticed that this prophecy has to do with the time of Messiah's coming.

(2) What happens to Messiah, the anointed, after threescore and two weeks (v. 26)? *He is cut off (or killed).* So the prophecy also mentions the death of Messiah.

(3) What is the purpose of the events related in this prophecy (v. 24)? *To make an end of sins, to make reconciliation for iniquity.*

(4) So Messiah's coming and death are related to sins and atonement.

b. This relationship is most clearly seen in Isaiah 52:13—53:12.

(1) Many of our religious leaders say this passage is talking about the nation Israel, but upon examination the passage doesn't indicate this.

(a) As we saw earlier, on the surface the passage appears to be describing an individual, who in 52:13-15 is described in terms used for Messiah.

(b) Who does "my people" refer to (53:8)? *Israel.* Correct, but if this whole passage is talking about Israel, then "my people" becomes meaningless. Someone is described as dying for the transgressions of Israel ("my people").

(c) Can Israel honestly be described as "having no violence, having no deceit in his mouth" (v. 9)? *No.* Isaiah said earlier (29:13) that Israel dishonored God with their mouths and claimed a relationship with God that they didn't have.

(d) In v. 10 the word for "recompense for guilt" is *asham* or "trespass offering." According to Leviticus 5 the trespass offering had to be perfect, without spot and without blemish. Can you say that Israel is without spot or blemish, perfect? Can they fit the qualifications of a trespass offering?

(e) The evidence from the passage itself indicates that an individual, the Messiah, is the subject of the prophecy.

(f) The Talmud affirms this when it says: "The Messiah—what is his name? . . . The rabbis say 'the leprous one'; those of the house of the rabbi say, 'the sick one,' as it is said, 'Surely he has borne our sicknesses' [Is 53:4]."[8]

(2) What did God cause to fall on the Messiah (v. 6)? *Our iniquities.* Iniquities is a synonym for sins.

(3) What did Messiah bear (v. 11)? *Iniquities.*

(4) Remember, in v. 10 "recompense for guilt" is the same word as "trespass offering." So Messiah's soul was made a trespass offering, an offering for sins.

(5) Because of Messiah's death, what did he take off (v. 12)? *The sin of many.*

(6) So Isaiah prophesied that Messiah would die to atone for our sins.

9. However, Messiah isn't left for dead; the Jewish prophets predicted his resurrection.

a. Psalm 16:10.

(1) The Hebrew term *azav,* translated "commit," carries the idea of "abandon" or "leave."

(2) Where won't God abandon the soul of his pious one? *The grave.*

(3) What won't the pious one see? *Corruption.* This term is not used to indicate moral corruption but bodily decay such as happens after death.

(4) Can this refer to David, who wrote this? *No, David died and was buried and his body decayed.* So this verse doesn't refer to David but to someone else. He is known as the "pious one," a designation for the Messiah. His body would not be left to decay in the grave. That means he would rise from the dead.

b. Isaiah 53:10 provides further evidence for this.

(1) As we have seen, Isaiah 53 refers to the death of Messiah to atone for sins.

(2) What does the phrase "he was cut off out of the land of the living (v. 8) mean? *He was killed.*

(3) What happens to the days of Messiah's life (last half of v. 10)? *They are prolonged.*

(4) But how can his life be prolonged if he has already died according to verses 8-9? *He must be raised from the dead.*

10. The coming of Messiah to the earth has been described by the prophets.

a. Many Jewish people believe the Messiah is to come in the future to bring peace and be a great political leader.

b. Zechariah 12:8-10 describes his coming.

(1) What will God do (v. 8)? *He will defend Israel.* Right, and in addition, the house of David will be exalted. Remember, Messiah is of the house of David.

(2) Who does Messiah destroy (v. 9)? *Israel's enemies.*

(3) What will he pour out on Israel (v. 10)? *The spirit of grace.*

(4) These verses describe events that will occur when Messiah comes. They are further described in chapters 12 and 13.

c. After Messiah has poured out the spirit of grace, what will the people do first (v. 10)? *Look to him.*

d. What will the people do after they look to him? *Mourn.*

e. Isn't it strange that the people would mourn at such a great event as the coming of Messiah? The answer to that may be found in how they recognize Messiah. Remember that italics are used to indicate words not found in the Hebrew text but supplied by the translator. Keeping this in mind, how is this one to whom the people look described? *The one whom they have pierced!* There is a visible appearance of a pierced, marred body.

f. When the Messiah comes as conqueror, the Jewish people will see that Messiah's body has wounds which he previously sustained. As the Talmud explains: "It is clear that it rather refers to Messiah . . . who was killed, for then we understand the whole verse which says: 'They shall look upon me whom they pierced.' "[9] No wonder the Jewish people are horror-struck and mourn bitterly over a previous misconception and wrong identification.

B. *The question of identification.*

Note: Don't make the identification of Messiah with Yeshua at any time during this sharing procedure. Let your Jewish friend do it. Prior to this point in your sharing, keep referring to what the Hebrew Scriptures teach. Say, for example, "We're just reading what the Hebrew Scriptures say about Messiah."

1. Whom do you think the prophets are describing?

2. Yeshua certainly meets the qualifications and fits the description of Messiah. If he was not the Messiah, then according to the Jewish Bible, Messiah must be someone just like Yeshua. He must fulfill all prophecies we've read plus others.[10]

3. What are the possibilities for a repeat of circumstances in which a Messiah could duplicate the life and ministry of Yeshua? It would be almost impossible to reset history to recreate conditions existing about 2000 years ago. This would require the birth of Messiah in Bethlehem, rejection by the people, his death to atone for sins and then his resurrection. Besides, the Messiah must come before the destruction of the Second Temple. Eventually, all Israel will recognize Messiah as the one who was pierced. In fact, the probability that one man could fulfill all these prophetic predictions is incredibly low (see pp. 124-25, section 9b).

4. The only intellectually honest interpretation of the historical data and the Hebrew Scriptures is that Yeshua is the Messiah of Israel.

C. *Here is what Yeshua claimed and offered.*

1. John 10:10—life in all its fullness. This means an abundant life, a victorious, supernatural and eternal life.

2. 2 Corinthians 5:17—a change in the individual's nature, a revolution of his character. He will completely change an individual's nature. Instead of hate and prejudice, there will be love; instead of indifference, deep concern for fellow man and a helping hand to those in need; instead of discord in relationships with others, harmony. These are changes which can permeate the whole of society.

3. John 14:27—peace, real shalom. He promises to give peace where it's most important, in the individual heart and mind. This is where peace must start if it is to spread through society. When an individual is at peace with himself and with God, he can share it with those around him.

4. Mark 10:45; Matthew 26:28—complete forgiveness of sins. Yeshua died to atone for sins. Now he promises forgiveness to those who respond to him and also promises a personal relationship with God.

D. *The Scriptures remind us (Is 62:11): "Behold the Lord has proclaimed to the end of the world, 'Say to the daughter of Zion, Behold your salvation [the Hebrew is Yeshua!] is coming; behold his reward is with him, and his work is before him.' " In light of this, how should a person respond to him? (Take him to point 5 in L'chaim.)*

How to Use National Prophecy
A. *Introduction.*
1. Frederick the Great (1712-86) once said to his chaplain, "Show me a miracle." The chaplain answered, "Sire, it is the Jews."
2. The miracle of the continued existence of the Jewish people through history is overshadowed only by another miracle, the fact that the history and survival of the Jewish people were accurately predicted many years ago by the great prophets of Israel.
3. During the time of these prophets, successful prophecy was not dabbling with the occult to find out about the future, educated guesswork or making more successful predictions than unsuccessful ones.
4. Deuteronomy 18:21-22. What is the standard which demonstrates that a prophet speaks for God? *His prophecies come true.* So the standard was 100% accuracy! If a prophet's predictions proved false, he was killed (v. 20).
5. Keeping this standard in mind, let's examine the predictions of the prophets of Israel about the history and survival of the Jewish people.
B. *Genesis 12:1-3; 17:1-8. God's program for Israel: his covenant with Abraham.*
1. Genesis 12:2.

a. What did God promise to make of Abraham? *A great nation.*

b. Which nation is this? *Israel.*

c. Abraham, and by implication the nation God would make of him, would be a source of what to the other nations of the earth (vv. 2-3)? *Blessing.*

2. Genesis 17:7.

a. With whom did God establish his covenant? *Abraham and his descendants.*

b. This covenant was confirmed to Isaac (Gen 17:19, 21) and to Jacob (Gen 25:23; 35:9-15).

3. How long was the covenant to be in effect? *Forever; it's an everlasting covenant.*

a. This covenant was given by God to guarantee the continuous existence of Abraham's descendants (through Isaac and Jacob) to the present day.

b. This is why the Jewish people exist today, despite repeated attempts to exterminate or assimilate them.

(1) There is only one logical explanation for the almost miraculous continuing existence of the Jews as a people. It is God's faithfulness to his promise to protect them and guarantee their existence as a people.

(2) Napoleon was asked by his marshals, who were atheists, if he believed there was a God. Napoleon pointed to Marshal Masena, a Jew, and said, "Gentlemen, there is the unmistakable argument that there is a God!"

c. As long as the human race continues, God promises that there will always be a Jewish people.

4. Genesis 17:8.

a. What did God promise to give Abraham and his descendants? *The land of Canaan (Palestine).*

b. How long would they have title to the land? *Forever; it's an everlasting possession.*

(1) This is the biblical and historical basis for the right to the land which the Jewish people claim.

(2) As long as there is a history of the human race, the Jewish people have the title deed to the land of Israel.

C. *God creates a nation.*

1. There are three essentials for nationhood: a people, a government and a homeland.

2. God insured Israel's distinctiveness and purity as a people by sending them to Egypt. (The story is told in Gen 46—Ex 12.)

a. Genesis 38:2. The sons of Jacob were intermingling with the Canaanites. There was a danger of assimilation and loss of identity.

b. So God saw to it that they went to Egypt. The Egyptians were separatists; they refused to intermarry; so the people of Israel maintained their identity. In Egypt they also multiplied in numbers large enough to be a nation, and over two million people left Egypt.

3. God then gave Israel a constitution as a nation and with it a government. This was the covenant with Israel through Moses (found in Ex 19—Lev 27, plus Deut).

a. This covenant told them how to live the totality of their lives before God; it spelled out the principles of maintaining a proper relationship with God and appropriating his blessings.

b. The covenant also included principles on how to govern themselves properly.

4. Then God gave Israel the homeland he promised to Abraham. Under Joshua, Israel entered and settled Canaan (see Josh 1—24).

D. *Leviticus 26:27-44; Deuteronomy 28:58-68. Prophecy concerning the history of Israel: the dark side.*

1. God issued a warning to Israel in Leviticus 26:27-28 (compare Deut 28:58).

a. What situation is described (v. 27)? *Not obeying God.*

b. What would be the result if Israel disobeyed God (v. 28)? *He would chastise (punish) them.*

2. Amos 2:4. The prophets continually warned Israel about their disobedience and God's impending judgment.

a. What won't God turn away or hold back? *Punishment.*

b. Why would God punish Israel? *Disobedience, despising God's law.*

c. The rest of the prophets continued to warn Israel about the promised consequences of disobeying God. (Compare Jer 14:2-13; Is 5:3-25, and others.) If you look at the messages of the prophets, you'll find that Israel continued to disobey God.

3. God promised certain things would happen if Israel disobeyed his commandments.

a. What would happen to the cities of Israel (Lev 26:31a)? *They would resemble waste or rubble.*

b. What would happen to the sanctuaries or sacred places of the Israelis (v. 31b)? *They would be desolate.*

c. What would be the condition of the land (v. 32a)? *Desolation.*

d. Who would inhabit the land (v. 32b)? *Israel's enemies.*

e. What would happen to the people of Israel (Deut 28:64a)? *They would be scattered throughout the earth.*

f. Where would God cause them to go again (v. 68a)? *Egypt.*

g. What would happen to them there (v. 68b)? *They would be sold as slaves.*

h. What will be the situation of the Jewish people as they live in foreign countries (vv. 65-66)? *They will suffer persecution.*

i. What would happen to many of the Jewish people when they were in foreign countries (Lev 26:38)? *Many would die.*

j. Despite the scattering, persecution and death, God promised to preserve the Jewish people through it all because of his covenant with Abraham (see Lev 26:11 and Deut 4:31).

4. All of these promises have come true.

a. The old cities of the Jewish people became heaps of rubble.

b. Their sacred places, including the Temple, were destroyed.

c. The land of Israel became like a desert.

d. Israel's enemies took over the land.

e. The Jewish people have been scattered among the nations of the world.

f. They were taken to Egypt in ships and sold as slaves in 70 CE.

g. The history of the Jewish people has been one of persecution and suffering.

h. Many Jewish people have died as a result of the persecution.

i. Yet through it all, miraculously, the Jewish people have survived and kept their identity.

j. So all of the prophecies we have read have been completely fulfilled; God has kept his promises.

E. *Isaiah 11:11-12; 35:1-2; Ezekiel 36:8, 12, 34; Amos 9:14; compare Jeremiah 23:7-8; 30:10-11; 31:8; 32:37-40; Ezekiel 11:17; 36:24. Prophecy concerning the history of Israel: the bright side.*

1. Isaiah 11:11-12.

a. What would God do a second time (v. 11)? *Regather the re-*

mainder of the Jewish people.
b. When was the first time God regathered the Jewish people? *After the captivity in Babylon.* The second time began in the 1860s and 1880s, increased between 1898 and 1948, accelerated in 1948 and is still going on now.
c. Where would the Jewish people come back from (v. 12)? *The four corners of the earth.* The Jewish people in Israel have come from the United States, South America, East and West Europe, Africa, Asia, the Arab countries and now Russia—in other words, from all over the earth.
2. Ezekiel 36:12.
a. In this passage God is speaking to the land. What would the Jewish people do with the land once they were in it? *Possess it; it would be their own land.*
b. From the 1860s until 1948, the Jewish people were allowed to immigrate to Palestine, but it wasn't their own land.
c. For almost two thousand years it appeared impossible that the Jewish people would ever have their own country again.
d. Finally, in 1948, what happened? *The nation of Israel was established.* Right, and the Jewish people had their country once again!
3. Amos 9:14.
a. What would happen to the ruined cities? *They'd be rebuilt and inhabited.*
b. The pictures of Israeli cities demonstrate this. Elath, En Gedi and Ashdod have been rebuilt and inhabited. Tel Aviv, Haifa and Jerusalem are modern metropolises.
4. Ezekiel 36:8.
a. What would happen on the mountains of Israel? *Trees would grow and produce.*
b. Before the Israelis began their reforestation program, the mountains of Israel were bare and eroded. Now about 200 million trees have been planted throughout the land.
5. Ezekiel 36:34.
a. What is said about the desolate desert land? *It would be tilled.*
b. The Arabs didn't cultivate the land of Palestine; they allowed it to remain mostly a desert. The Israelis have cultivated the desert land through the process of irrigation. It is just as Isaiah predicted

(35:6). There are "waters in the wilderness and streams in the desert."

6. Isaiah 35:1-2.

a. What was to happen to the desert? *It would blossom like a rose.*

b. Pictures of Israel show that where there was once dry, parched desert, there are now green, fertile plains. In fact, exporting of roses has become a multimillion-dollar business.

c. Through the process of atomic irrigation, the Israelis brought the land to life so that now a major source of income in Israel is agriculture.

7. All of these prophecies were written before 500 BCE. Yet each of them has been specifically fulfilled in the history of Israel just as predicted.

F. *Transition.*

1. Isn't it amazing the way the prophets spelled out the details of the history of Israel before the events ever happened?

2. It should make a person proud to be Jewish, to be part of the nation God has kept his hand on throughout history.

3. The fulfillment of such specific prophecies makes it difficult to deny that God was behind these prophecies, fulfilling his promises to the Jewish people.

4. It should make us more curious to read the Bible and let it speak to us. We ought to know what the Bible says because it is a valid source of information and should command our respect.

5. You know, the Bible also has something to say about Israel's future.

G. *The prophetic outlook for Israel: the future.*

1. As we have seen already, the prophecies concerning Israel's future have both a bleak and a bright side.

2. Jeremiah 30:4-7 talks of a time of trouble ahead for Israel.

3. Zechariah 13:8-9 describes this time in drastic terms.

a. What fraction of the people of Israel will be cut off and die (v. 8)? *Two-thirds.*

b. According to verse 9 God uses this time of intense suffering to refine the character of the remaining one-third of the Jewish people and to bring them into a personal relationship with himself.

c. Apparently there lies ahead for the nation Israel a time of intense anti-Jewishness on a worldwide basis. Some of this pressure will come from various power blocks that will move into the Middle East. This has also been predicted by the Bible prophets, but it forms part of a separate discussion.

4. However, God will preserve the people of Israel through all this destruction.

a. Zechariah 13:9b. Under these desperate conditions, what will the remaining Jewish people do? *They'll call on God for help.* Yes, and he will intervene to help them.

b. Zechariah 14:3-4. This has always been considered a Messianic passage. Messiah will come at this time to deliver his people from destruction and to rule them (compare Zech 12:7-9).

c. Zechariah 12:10 describes the coming of Messiah.

(1) What does he pour out on the people? *Spirit of grace and supplication.*

(2) Isaiah 59:20-21 indicates that the spirit of grace and supplication which is poured out is a sign that Messiah has inaugurated the covenant described by Jeremiah and Ezekiel.

5. The covenant of Jeremiah 31:30-39 (compare Ezek 36:24-27).

a. Verses 37-39 describe a restored and expanded city of Jerusalem, the center of Messiah's rule.

b. What kind of covenant is described (v. 30)? *A new one.*

c. What is this covenant not according to or not like (v. 31)? *The covenant given through Moses.* In other words, God has something new in mind for the Jewish people.

d. There are some radical spiritual and moral aspects of this new covenant.

(1) What will God cause to be written in men's hearts to be an integral part of their natures (v. 32)? *His law.* This will mean that everyone will respond properly to God spontaneously and naturally.

(2) What two thoughts describe a personal and proper relationship with God (v. 33b)? *Knowing God and having forgiveness of sins.*

e. One of the greatest benefits that Messiah will inaugurate as part of the new covenant is this intimate, unhindered relationship with God. This will result in a life that can be lived to the utmost for God and man.

6. Zechariah 12:10 gives a most interesting description of Messiah as he institutes these great benefits.

a. Words printed in italics indicate words not in the Hebrew text but supplied by the translator.

b. The people of Israel will look to Messiah. As they look to him, how is he described? *The pierced one.*

c. This has always been regarded as a passage describing the coming of Messiah (see the Talmud, Sukkah 52a). Yet the deliverer of Israel is described as the "pierced one." Psalm 22:16 and Isaiah 53:5 are other descriptions of Messiah as the "pierced one."

d. How do the Jewish people react to the coming of Messiah? *They'll mourn.* The Jewish people will be in mourning as a result of this startling revelation that the Messiah is the one who was pierced for their sins when he was here the first time.

H. *Before his return to earth, the Messiah, "the pierced one," is making available the tremendous life and relationship with God described in the new covenant of Jeremiah 31. (Go to a presentation of L'chaim or one of the other approaches in this chapter.)*

How to Use End-Time Prophecy
A. *Introduction.*

1. Recently *The Global 2000 Report to the President* (based on the findings of thirteen government agencies) issued a grim warning. "If present trends continue, the world in 2000 will be more crowded, more polluted, less stable ecologically, and more vulnerable to disruption than the world we live in now."[11]

2. To this, one may add the conclusions of the Club of Rome, a highly respected international body consisting of a hundred scientists, educators, economists, industrialists and various civil servants. They predict "the total breakdown and collapse of the world system as we know it by early to mid 21st century if nothing is done about the problems we now face."[12] Two factors heighten the urgency of the Club's observations. While taking into consideration population, consumption, industrialization, pollution and the earth's raw materials and resources, the Club largely ignored the effects of political and social upheaval. They also pointed out that if a cooperative global effort to deal with the world's problems was not well under way by the early 1980s, the situation may well be irreversible.

3. Centuries ago the prophets of Israel predicted the same kind of crisis and they described some of the events and forces that would lead to such a crisis. Their predictions are found in the Jewish Bible.

B. *One of the most important events in the time period leading up to the crisis is found in Isaiah 11:11-12.*

1. What will the Lord do a second time (v. 11)? *Recover the remnant of his people; that is, bring the Jewish people back to Israel.* The first time the Lord did this was after the captivity of the Jews in Babylon. When did the second time begin? *In 1948.*

2. Where will the Jewish people come from (v. 12)? *The four corners of the earth.* The Jewish people have returned to Israel from North and South America, Eastern and Western Europe, Africa, Asia, the Arab countries and, most recently, Russia—truly from all over the earth.

C. *Zechariah 12:2-3. After Israel becomes a national entity again, it will occupy the attention of the world.*

1. What will God make Jerusalem and Israel at this time (v. 3)? *A burdensome stone.*

2. To whom will Israel be a burden? *All peoples.* In other words, Israel will be the center of trouble and concern for the entire world. Sounds like today's headlines, doesn't it?

D. *Several nations or groups of nations will have a deep interest in this situation. The first of these nations is described in Ezekiel 38: 1-2, 15-16.*

1. Who is this prophecy directed against (v. 1)? *Gog.*

2. What places is he prince of (v. 2)? *Rosh, Meshech and Tubal.*

3. Where will he come from (v. 15)? *From his place in the north parts.* This is better translated "from the remote parts of the north." What nation could be described as the remote parts of the north in relation to Israel? *Russia.*

4. What will he do (v. 16a)? *Come against Israel.*

5. Dr. Wilhelm Gesenius traced back these ancient tribal terms to determine to whom they referred. He discovered that Tubal is now known as Tobolsk, the former eastern capital of Russia. In Greek, Meshech was called Moschi and is now called Moscow. Rosh was the name given to a tribe of people living between the Ural Mountains and the Baltic Sea and is the term from which we get Russia.[13]

6. So Ezekiel predicted that Russia would be one of Israel's eneies during these times.

E. *Daniel 11:40, 43. A group of nations is mentioned in connection with Israel.*

1. Who will push into Israel (v. 40)? *The King of the south.* Apparently this refers to the leader of a federation of nations south of Israel.

2. What are some of the nations that are part of this federation (v. 43)? *Egypt, Libya and Ethiopia.*

3. The Hebrew word for Libya is *Phut.* It refers not only to Libya but also to the surrounding North African Arab nations.

4. The Hebrew word for Ethiopia is *Cush.* It too refers to an area broader than Ethiopia and includes many of the Black African nations.

5. Therefore, Daniel predicts the involvement of Egypt and the Arab and African nations at this time.

F. *Daniel 11:44. Daniel also makes a passing reference to another group of nations that will take an interest in Israel.*

What will trouble him? *Tidings out of the east and north. Apparently a group of nations east of Israel will begin to take an active interest in the area. We'll talk about these nations from the east a little later.*

G. *Daniel 7:23-24. Daniel used symbolic language to refer to another confederation of nations that would be forming about this time.*

1. What does the fourth beast represent (v. 23)? *The fourth kingdom to rule the earth.*

2. This fourth kingdom that will rule the earth can be identified by comparing Daniel 2 and 7, the historical setting of Daniel and subsequent world history. From Daniel's perspective the fourth kingdom was the Roman Empire.

3. What would arise out of the remnants of the Roman Empire (v. 24)? *Ten kings.* They represent ten kingdoms of nations, apparently forged into a federation, and coming from the areas which were part of the old Roman Empire.

4. We don't see this federation presently, but we may see the foundation for it.

a. *Time* magazine in a 4 July 1969 article, "Europe's Dreams of

Unity Revive," made a significant statement: "Should all go according to the most optimistic schedules, the Common Market could someday expand into a ten-nation economic unity whose industrial might would far surpass that of the Soviet Union."

b. In 1983 the Common Market included ten member nations. If you examine the geographic area covered by these ten nations, the area roughly corresponds to that included in the Roman Empire.

H. *Daniel 7:24. A very significant development will occur within this ten-nation federation.*

1. Who will arise after the ten kings? *Another king.*

2. What will he do? *Subdue three of the kings.* Afterward he assumes the leadership of the federation.

3. A comparison of chapter 11:40-45 with this passage clearly shows that this leader of the ten-nation federation will have immense power.

4. An unidentified European leader said in connection with the Common Market, "The final aim is political unity; and when this end is realized, a genius must be found to head it up."

5. Or as another European leader put it, "This man we need and for whom we wait will take charge of the defense of the West. Once more I say, it is not too late, but it is high time."

6. The stage seems set for another of the prophets' predictions to come true.

I. *Jeremiah 23:1-8 and Zechariah 12–14. As we've seen, the Jewish prophets painted an accurate picture of what would take place in the times of impending crisis. However, they also predicted the intervention of a powerful, godly figure to set the situation straight.*

1. Whom will God raise up (Jer 23:5)? *A descendant (sprout) of David.*

2. What will his function be? *To reign as king.*

3. Who is this person (vv. 5-6)? *Messiah.*

4. His coming is described in Zechariah. After Messiah pours out the spirit of grace on Israel, what do the people do (12:10)? *They look to him.*

5. What do they do next? *They mourn.*

6. Isn't it strange that when they should be celebrating, the people of Israel are mourning? The answer might be found in the way the people recognize him.

7. Words in italics indicate words supplied by the translator but not found in the Hebrew text. Keeping this in mind, tell how the people recognize Messiah when they look to him. *As the one whom they have pierced!* In other words, the Jewish people will see, in Messiah's body, wounds that he sustained at a previous coming.

J. *There is a person in history who fits this description of Messiah, Yeshua of Nazareth. He claimed to be Messiah (Jn 4:25-26), and many people believed that claim (Acts 6:7). He said he would return during the time of crisis and would reign as Messiah the king (Mt 24:3–25:46). He mentioned some specific events that would serve as indicators of his coming.*

K. *Yeshua predicted some very significant events in the history of Israel.*

1. When Jerusalem is surrounded by enemies, what will happen next to the nation Israel (Lk 21:20)? *It will be desolate; that is, the nation will be destroyed.*

2. What will happen to the people (v. 24)? *They will be killed or taken captive.*

3. What will be the extent of their captivity or scattering? *Throughout all the nations.*

4. This was fulfilled first in 70 CE and finally in 135 CE.

5. Prior to Yeshua's return, where will the Jewish people be once again (Mt 24:16)? *In Judea.* Judea covers almost the same area as modern Israel.

6. So Yeshua is indicating that the Jewish people would return to their land before his return. When did this first take place? *In May 1948.*

L. *Yeshua predicted that several things would occur in and around Jerusalem prior to his return.*

1. What will Israel's enemies do after they surround Jerusalem (Lk 19:43-44)? *They will level Jerusalem.*

2. This prediction came true in 70 CE when Titus and the Roman legions destroyed Jerusalem and the Temple.

3. How long will Jerusalem be controlled (trampled underfoot) by the Gentiles (Lk 21:24)? *Until the times of the Gentiles are fulfilled.* The period of Gentile domination over Jerusalem will end, and the Jewish people will once again control the city.

4. When was this prophecy fulfilled? *June 1967.*

M. *Yeshua also predicted several things about the Temple in Jerusalem.*
1. What would happen to the Temple buildings (Mt 24:1-2)? *They'll be torn down completely.*
2. Just before Yeshua's return, where will the abomination of desolation stand (Mt. 24:15)? *In the holy place.*
3. What does the holy place refer to? *The Temple.*
4. So Yeshua predicted that the Temple would be rebuilt prior to his return.
5. The Chief Rabbi of Israel, Shlomo Goren, said in an interview for the March 1974 issue of the *Times of Israel:* "I believe we will have to establish a Third Temple in modern Israel. . . . The Third Temple will come in our time. It is part and parcel of our Messianic tradition."
N. *Yeshua also made some predictions about the international situation prior to his return.*
1. There would be a constant threat of what (Mt 24:6-7)? *War and fighting.*
2. According to "A World at War—1983," a report of the Center for Defense Information, a group headed by retired senior U.S. military officers, "Forty-five nations, more than one-fourth of those in the world, are now engaged in wars, and some of the conflicts could lead to direct nuclear confrontation between the United States and the Soviet Union" (*St. Petersburg Times,* 20 March 1983, p. 26-A).
3. Earlier we talked about a group of nations from the East getting involved in the Middle East.
4. Why will the Euphrates River be dried up (Rev 16:12)? *To prepare the way for the kings from the east.* The term *east* literally means "rising of the sun" and was the ancient designation for the Oriental nations.
5. So a federation of Oriental nations will make its presence felt in the Middle East during this crisis period.
6. Revelation 9:13-18 apparently describes the armies of the eastern federation (v. 16). How many men are involved? *200 million.* According to a *Time* magazine article of 21 May 1966, "It is now estimated that Red China has an army of 200 million."
7. The *Mexico City News* of 2 July 1971, reported the construction

of a road linking China's westernmost province with the Pakistani part of Karachi. The article continued, "For China the road represents a strategic victory in the battle for world trade, a short-cut outlet to the Arabian Sea and the Indian Ocean and access to the Middle East." The stage seems set.

O. *Another of Yeshua's predictions had to do with physical circumstances preceding his return.*

1. What will occur in numerous places (Mt 24:7)? *Famines and earthquakes.*

2. According to *The Global 2000 Report to the President*, the number of malnourished worldwide will increase from a half-billion people in the mid 1970s to 1.3 billion by 2000, with starvation claiming increasing numbers of babies. Due to overuse and other factors such as loss of topsoil, farming land will become less fertile, further aggravating the world's food shortage problems.

A UN-financed report adds "that only dramatic shifts in population policy will avert famine and severe economic hardship in many parts of the globe" (*St. Petersburg Times*, 27 March 1983, p.21-A).

3. Over a recent two-year period, the *Chicago Tribune* failed to report an earthquake somewhere in the world on only four days. The first measurable earthquake in Colorado's history took place in March 1962. During the next six years there were 1600. Reports about earthquakes have now become almost a regular feature of our newspapers.

P. *Yeshua also predicted some social signs that would precede his return.*

1. What would be on the increase (Mt 24:12)? *Lawlessness.*

2. According to the FBI's "Uniform Crime Report," serious crimes took place at a level 55% higher in 1980 than a decade before. In fact, the 1980 crime increase was four times the increase in population (*Chicago Sun-Times*, 11 September 1981, p. 25).

Q. *These certainly are good indications that the Jewish prophets and Yeshua the Messiah knew what they were talking about. However, they also had some important things to say about man's life and destiny. Let's take a look at them. (Go through L'chaim.)*

How to Present the Principles of Having a Relationship with God

A. *Introduction*

1. Relationships are an essential part of human life as we know it. Having good relationships with others is a sign of psychological and emotional maturity.

2. But one relationship is more important than the rest, and it is vital that this one be good. It is man's relationship with God.

3. Our rabbis have taught us that prayer, repentance and mitzvot (good deeds) form the foundation of a good relationship with God. These are important, but the Jewish Scriptures teach us more.

B. *God requires certain things from us.*

1. Deuteronomy 6:4-5. What are we expected to do? *Love God with all our hearts, souls, and might.*

2. Deuteronomy 10:12-13. What else does God require? *Fear God, walk in all his ways, love him, serve him with all our hearts and souls, keep his commandments.*

3. Let's go back to Deuteronomy 6:1-2.

a. How many of God's commandments are we to keep (v. 2)? *All of them.*

b. For how long? *All the days of our lives.*

4. Leviticus 19:2 adds one more thing. What is expected of us? *To be holy like God is.*

5. In all honesty, can you consistently live this kind of life, meeting these standards? *No.*

C. *Our Scriptures indicate that everyone faces this same problem.*

1. Isaiah 64:5a. Because of his absolute holiness, how does God view all of us and our good deeds, called "righteousness" here? *As an unclean thing and filthy garments.* This conveys God's perspective of our best efforts in comparison with his holiness, his standard.

2. Since this is the case, the Jewish Bible makes an accurate observation.

a. Ecclesiastes 7:20. What is that observation? *There isn't a just man on earth that does good and doesn't sin.*

b. Psalm 143:2. Why does the author request that God not enter into judgment with him? *No man living can be justified in God's sight.* Justified means being considered righteous or being regarded in right relationship by God.

3. We are forced to conclude then that we have all broken God's standards and are guilty in his sight.
D. *God is absolutely holy and just. Because we have violated his standards, he must deal with these violations.*
1. Habakkuk 1:13. How does God react to evil and the breaking of his laws? *Can't look on or tolerate it.*
2. Ezekiel 33:12-13. God's absolute holiness as reflected in this passage explains why God responds as he does.
a. When won't the righteousness of righteous men be sufficient (v. 12)? *When they sin.*
b. What happens when a person trusts in his own righteousness and commits sin (v. 13)? *His righteousness won't be remembered.*
c. What will happen because of the sin he has committed (v. 13)? *He will die for it.* See also Jeremiah 31:29. Death here involves not merely physical death but spiritual separation from God as well, as is described in Isaiah 59:2.
3. Nahum 1:3. Because of his character, can God simply overlook these things and acquit the wicked or guilty parties? *No, God doesn't acquit the wicked.* See also Exodus 34:7.
E. *Remember that, according to Deuteronomy 6 and 10, God expects us to love and serve him with all our hearts.*
1. Jeremiah 17:9. But we all have a basic problem. How is man's heart described? *Deceitful above all things and desperately sick.* So our hearts can't deliver what God desires.
2. Psalm 51:12. David recognized this. What was his request? *That God create a clean heart in him.*
3. Ezekiel 11:19-20.
a. What does God do to give us clean hearts (v. 19)? *Takes out our stony hearts and replaces them with hearts of flesh.*
b. Why does he do this (v. 20)? *So we can walk in his statutes and keep his ordinances (commandments).*
4. Elsewhere this process is described as God's "circumcising the heart" (Deut 30:6), "putting his laws in the heart" (Jer 31:32), or "giving men a new heart" (Ezek 36:26). These phrases picture what God does to make our hearts right.
F. *In order to discover on what basis God works in our hearts and lives, we can observe how he has worked in the history of our people.*

1. Deuteronomy 7:6-8. God's election or choosing of the Jewish people.
a. Was God's choice based on Israel's merit or special qualifications such as size (v. 7)? *No. They lacked these.*
b. What was it based on (v. 8)? *God's love and faithfulness* (compare Deut 4:37; 10:15).
2. The deliverance from Egypt and the possession of the promised land illustrate this point.
a. Deuteronomy 9:5a. What things are not reasons for God's allowing them to possess the land? *Not for their righteousness or uprightness of heart.*
b. How are the people described (vv. 6-7)? *Stiffnecked (stubborn) and rebellious.* (Compare Deuteronomy 31:27.)
c. Psalm 106:6. What had the people done? *Sinned, committed iniquity, did wickedly.*
d. Despite all this why did God act on their behalf (v. 8)? *For his name's sake and to make his power known.* Compare vv. 43-45.
e. God's action in the Exodus and the conquest of the Promised Land was therefore certainly not based on Israel's goodness or merit. It was based on God's character and mercy.
3. God's acting in love and mercy, apart from merit, in a way that is undeserved by the recipient, is called grace (Hebrew *hen*, sometimes also described by *hesed*). Grace also describes the way in which God deals with man's sin.
a. Psalm 51:3. On what basis does David request God to blot out transgressions, on David's effort or merit? *No.* Why then? *Because of God's loving-kindness and tender mercy.* (See also Psalm 86:13.)
b. Psalm 25:7. According to what does David ask God not to remember his sins? *God's mercy and for his goodness' sake.*
c. Why should God pardon iniquity (v. 11)? *For his name's sake.*
d. Isaiah 43:25. How does God describe himself? *As the one who blots out transgressions for his own sake.*
e. "For his own sake" and "for his name's sake" are common ways of describing God's action when what he does is undeserved, done out of grace.
4. The covenant or contract God made with Abraham further amplifies how God acts in grace. The covenant is always presented as God's spontaneous action. The initiative is always his (compare

Neh 9:7). The frequently repeated phrase "for his name's sake" is a reminder that the covenant operates continually, not for what God's people are but for what he is.

a. Genesis 12:1-3. Who is viewed as the initiator of the relationship and the blessings? *God.* Note the repeated use of "I."

b. Is the blessing based on anything Abraham did here? *No. Nothing is mentioned.*

c. Deuteronomy 10:15. Why did God choose Abraham and bless him? *Out of love.* So God is acting out of grace once again.

d. Genesis 15. God repeats and enlarges his promises to Abraham (vv. 4-7). In verse 8 Abraham asks how he is to know that these promises will come true.

(1) What does God tell him to do (v. 9)? *Take a heifer, she-goat, ram, turtledove and pigeon.*

(2) What did Abraham do with the animals (v. 10)? *Divided them and laid one piece against the other.*

(3) What passed between the pieces (v. 17)? *Smoking furnace, burning flame.* This is similar to the pillar of fire which represented God's presence in leading the Jewish people out of Egypt and through the desert (Ex 13:21); it represents God's presence.

(4) What did the Lord do that day (v. 18a)? *Made a covenant with Abraham.*

(5) In Abraham's time there was a specific procedure for ratifying a contract or covenant. The contracting parties sacrificed certain animals, divided the pieces in half on the ground (vv. 9-10) and walked between the pieces (v. 17). This made the contract official and binding (v. 18). Here, only God walked between the pieces and assumed the responsibility for the contract.

e. So God's covenant with Abraham was initiated by God's own love and grace and was confirmed by a sacrifice. God's love was to motivate obedience on Abraham's part, in this case, circumcision and faithfulness to God (Gen 17:9-10; 18:18-19).

5. The contract or covenant God made through Moses at Mt. Sinai follows the same principles.

a. Exodus 19:4-8 describes the making of this covenant. What is the covenant based on (v. 4)? *God's delivering the people during the Exodus.*

b. Deuteronomy 7:8. Why did God do all this? *Because he loved*

them (compare Psalm 106:6, 8).
c. Exodus 24:4-8 describes the confirming or ratifying of this covenant.
(1) After he wrote down all the words of the covenant, what did Moses do (v. 4)? *Built an altar.*
(2) What did he have the young men do (v. 5)? *Offer sacrifices.*
(3) What did he do with the terms of the contract, the book of the covenant (v. 7)? *Read them to the people.*
(4) What was their response? *All the Lord said, we will do.*
(5) How did Moses seal the contract (v. 8)? *Sprinkled the blood of the sacrifice on the people.* This was the customary way of making a contract binding (compare Ps 50:5).
d. So God's covenant with Israel, as with Abraham, was initiated by God's love and grace and confirmed by sacrifices. It also included sacrifices as part of the covenant (see Leviticus). God's love was to motivate love and obedience on Israel's part, love for God and faithfulness to his instructions (Ex 19:4-6).
e. The rabbis understood this and pointed out that keeping the commandments, performing the mitzvot, followed from a relationship with God. Mitzvot did not precede or produce the relationship. The Talmud indicates this: "Why does the section 'Hear, O Israel' precede 'And it shall come to pass if ye shall hearken'?— So that a man may first take upon him the yoke of the kingdom of heaven and afterwards take upon the yoke of the commandments."[14]
6. The basis of relationship with God, as shown by Israel's history, is God's grace in freely entering into a covenant, pledging himself to show his favor and thus calling for a response of love and obedience, and then ratifying the covenant with a sacrifice.
G. *Sacrifices may seem crude and uncivilized to us. Sacrificial systems were not unique to Israel but are practically universal in ancient and primitive societies. Somehow man sensed that he was out of step with God, that something was wrong. He felt the need to conciliate God in some way, and sacrifices filled this role. This insight into sinfulness, illustrated by the universal presence of sacrificial systems, should cause us to question our modern age, which is the only age that hasn't recognized the seriousness of the problem.*[15]
1. In Israel's sacrificial system, it was seen that man's sin produced

a spiritual separation from God leading to physical death and total separation from God. Yet there was hope that a righteous God could still forgive sin. A sacrifice was made as a substitute for the sinner.

2. As the sacrifice was killed, the graphic reality of the horror of sin impressed itself on the offerer because it pictured the end of a sinful life as destruction. The offerer would place his hand on the sacrifice animal, symbolically identifying with the animal. It was as if he were saying, "Before a holy God, I've sinned; his perfection and holiness should cause him to reject me for my sin. His rejection is death. What I deserve is to die as this animal. Yet, somehow, God says that he will accept this animal in my place." This very act of sacrifice, if carried out sincerely, was a concrete expression of repentance and formed the basis of acceptance by God. The sacrifices were thus said to make atonement (see Lev 17:11).

3. The Hebrew term for atonement (kipper) conveys the same idea. It means "to ransom by means of a substitute." In other words, God's just punishment for sin was averted by an appropriate sacrifice. This accomplished a reconciliation between God and man.

4. The importance of the sacrifice system was consistently recognized by the ancient rabbis. For example, the Jerusalem Talmud, Makkot 31d, states:

They asked Wisdom (Hagiographa), "What is the punishment of the sinner?" Wisdom answered, "Evil pursues sinners" [Prov 13:21]. They asked Prophecy, "What is the punishment of the sinner?" Prophecy answered, "The soul that sinneth, it shall die" [Ezek 18:4]. They asked the Torah, "What is the punishment of the sinner?" Torah answered, "Let him bring a guilt offering and it shall be forgiven unto him, as it is said, 'and it shall be accepted for him to make atonement for him' " (Lev 1:4).

H. *There is still one more covenant that God instituted that helps us understand the way he changes men's hearts to bring them into a proper relationship with himself.*

1. Several prophets described this covenant.

a. Jeremiah 31:30-31. What is this covenant called? *A new covenant, not like the one made before at Sinai.*

b. At whose initiative is the new covenant made? *God's* (indicated by the repeated use of *I*).

c. So God initiates this covenant, just as he did the previous ones, out of his love and grace (see v. 36).

d. What will God do as part of the new covenant (v. 32a)? *Put his law in our inward parts and write it in our hearts.* Notice his work in our hearts.

e. What else will he do (v. 33b)? *Forgive our sins.*

f. Ezekiel 36:26 is another description of this new covenant. How is God's action described here? *Giving us a new heart and spirit, taking away our stony heart and replacing it with one of flesh.*

g. What is the end result of God's action (v. 27)? *Putting his spirit in us and our keeping his commandments and walking in his statutes.*

h. Therefore, through this new covenant God produces the necessary changes in people's hearts to enable them to be in right relationship with him and to live as he desires. As with the other covenants, God institutes this covenant in grace, thereby motivating a response of love and obedience. The other covenants were confirmed by sacrifices; this element seems to be missing here.

2. The answer to this problem also provides the clue to how the new covenant takes effect in the lives of individuals.

a. Daniel 9:25. Whose coming is predicted? *The anointed, the prince.* "Anointed" is the translation of the Hebrew term *mashiach*, "Messiah."

b. What is part of the purpose of Messiah's coming (v. 24)? *To finish transgression, make an end of sin, make reconciliation for iniquity, bring in everlasting righteousness.*

c. These descriptions are similar to Messiah's functions as we've always known them from passages such as Isaiah 4:2-5 and 11:1-10. They also describe the effects the new covenant will produce. They speak of that great time on earth when Messiah will rule and the knowledge of God will fill the earth. This is one set of images of the Messiah; there are others as well.

d. Zechariah 9:9. Why is Israel (Zion) to rejoice? *Her king is coming.* This has consistently been regarded as a description of Messiah's coming, Messiah being the king.

e. How is he described? *Just and lowly, riding an ass.* A great king usually rides a horse, yet Messiah is pictured riding on a donkey. This is the author's way of describing Messiah's humiliation and lowliness at his coming.

f. Daniel 9 adds a startling fact amplifying the humiliation and lowliness of Messiah. What happens to Messiah (the anointed) in verse 26a? *He's cut off.* Yes, he's killed!

3. The prophet Isaiah goes into more detail about Messiah's death. Chapters 52:13—53:12 form a major passage on Messiah, a passage which was recognized as Messianic from our earliest history following its writing. It's only been relatively recently that some scholars have tried to set aside its Messianic interpretation.[16]

a. A study of the passage itself shows that it is intended to describe the Messiah.

(1) 52:13-15 describes a person the way Isaiah usually describes the Messiah (for example, in 42:1; 49:6).

(2) Singular pronouns are used throughout, describing a person who is often contrasted with the people, i.e., Israel.

(3) The person is described in terms inappropriate for Israel or anyone but the Messiah: "had done no violence," "no deceit in his mouth," "silent before his tormentors."

b. What has God caused to happen to him (v. 6)? *All our iniquity to fall on him.* Verse 5 says he was "wounded for our transgressions." The Hebrew for "wounded" *(chalal)* literally means "pierced."

c. Why was he killed (cut off—v. 8)? *Because of the transgressions of my people.*

d. By his death, what did Messiah take off (v. 12b)? *The sin of many.*

e. If he has died (v. 8), how can his days be prolonged (v. 10b)? *He'd have to come back from the dead.* In other words, he is resurrected.

f. Therefore, the reason Messiah died was to atone for our sins. That means his death is the sacrifice that confirms or ratifies the new covenant! His death makes it possible for us to experience its blessings and have the new hearts necessary to properly obey God. And his resurrection is the validation of all he's done.

4. Zechariah the prophet provides confirmation of this. In a passage long regarded as Messianic, he pictures the coming of Messiah.

a. Zechariah 12:8. What will God do in that day? *Defend Israel from her enemies.*

b. What will Israel do in this time of great things, the coming of

Messiah (v. 10b, read from "they shall mourn")? *They'll mourn.*
Isn't that strange? When people should be extremely happy because Messiah is here, they're sad.
c. Verse 10a provides the answer. Words printed in italics are the
editor's way of showing that those words are not in the original
text. Keeping this in mind, describe the one to whom the people
look. *The one who was pierced!*
d. In other words, when Messiah comes, there are the visible
marks of his having been pierced at a previous coming. No wonder
the people mourn over their previous misunderstanding and mis-
identification.
5. Therefore, the new covenant which God makes to give us the
new hearts we need to be right with him is ratified by Messiah's
sacrifice. And it is that sacrifice for sins that makes atonement for
us. All that remains is for us to take advantage of it. (Go through
L'chaim.)

How to Present the Resurrection
1. The Jewish prophets of the Bible predicted many things about
the Messiah. These serve as identifying marks. One of the most
outstanding is the resurrection of the Messiah. Both Isaiah (53:10)
and David (Ps 16:10) make reference to this event which, perhaps
above all others, helps us identify the Messiah.
2. Throughout history only one person's claim to resurrection has
had any evidence to substantiate it. That person is Yeshua from
Nazareth. He claimed to be Israel's Messiah. When questioned, he
asserted that his resurrection from the dead would be the ultimate
proof of his Messiahship and deity.
3. He was executed: three days later hsi grave was empty.
4. The following article by Josh McDowell clearly explains the
evidence for affirming that Yeshua was raised from the dead.

The Case of the Empty Tomb
Eyewitness Accounts.   Some of the facts relevant to the resurrection are as follows: Yeshua of Nazareth, a Jewish prophet who
claimed to be the Messiah prophesied in the Jewish Scriptures,
was arrested, judged a political criminal and crucified. Three
days after his death and burial some women who went to his tomb

found the body gone. His disciples claimed that God had raised him from the dead and that he had appeared to them various times before ascending into heaven.

Did the resurrection actually happen? Was the tomb of Yeshua really empty? Controversy over these questions continues to rage even today.

The New Testament accounts of the resurrection were being circulated within the lifetimes of those alive at the time of the resurrection. These people could certainly confirm or deny the accuracy of these accounts.

Those who wrote the four Gospels either had themselves been witnesses or else had related the accounts of eyewitnesses of the actual events. In advocating their case for the gospel, the apostles had appealed (even when confronting their most severe opponents) to common knowledge concerning the facts of the resurrection.[17]

F. F. Bruce, the Rylands professor of biblical criticism and exegesis at the University of Manchester, says concerning the value of the New Testament records as primary sources: "Had there been any tendency to depart from the facts in any material respect, the possible presence of hostile witnesses in the audience would have served as a further corrective."[18]

Reliability of Sources. Because the New Testament provides the primary historical source for information on the resurrection, many critics during the 19th century attacked the reliability of these documents.

F. C. Bauer assumed that the New Testament Scriptures were not written until late in the second century A.D. He concluded that these writings came basically from myths or legends that had developed during the lengthy interval between the lifetime of Yeshua and the time these accounts were set down in writing.

By the end of the 19th century, however, archaeological discoveries had confirmed the accuracy of the New Testament manuscripts. Discoveries of early papyri manuscripts bridged the gap between the time of Yeshua and existing manuscripts from a later date.

These findings increased scholarly confidence in the reliability of the Bible. William Albright, who was the world's foremost biblical archaeologist, said: "We can already say emphatically that there is no longer any solid basis for dating any book of the New Testament after about A.D. 80, two full generations before the date between 130 and 150 given by the more radical New Testament critics of today.[19]

14,000 Manuscript Copies. Coinciding with the papyri discoveries, an abundance of other manuscripts came to light (over 14,000 copies of early New Testament manuscripts are known to be in existence today).[20] This motivated Sir Frederick Kenyon, one of the leading authorities on the reliability of ancient manuscripts, to write:

> The interval then between the dates of the original composition and the earliest extant evidence becomes so small as to be in fact negligible, and the last foundation for any doubt that the Scriptures have come down to us substantially as they were written has now been removed. Both the authenticity and the general integrity of the books of the New Testament may be regarded as finally established.[21]

The historian Luke wrote of "authentic evidence" concerning the resurrection.[22] Sir William Ramsay, who spent 15 years attempting to undermine Luke's credentials as a historian and to refute the reliability of the New Testament, finally concluded: "Luke is a historian of the first rank.... This author should be placed along with the very greatest of historians."[23]

Burial of Yeshua. The New Testament witnesses well knew the circumstances of the resurrection. The body of Yeshua, in accordance with the Jewish custom of burial, was wrapped in a linen cloth. About 100 pounds of aromatic spices, mixed together to form a gummy substance, were applied to the wrappings of cloth about the body.[24]

After the body was placed in a solid rock tomb, [25] an extremely large stone was rolled against the entrance of the tomb.[26] Large stones weighing approximately two tons were normally rolled (by means of levers) against a tomb entrance.

A Roman guard of strictly disciplined fighting men was stationed to guard the tomb. Fear of punishment "produced flawless attention to duty, especially in the night watches."[27]

This Roman guard affixed on the tomb the Roman seal, a stamp of Roman power and authority.[28] The Roman seal affixed thereon was meant to prevent any attempted vandalizing of the sepulcher. Anyone trying to move the stone from the tomb's entrance would have broken the seal and thus incurred the wrath of Roman law. *The Empty Tomb.* But the tomb was empty. The followers of Yeshua said he had risen from the dead. They reported that he appeared to them during a period of 40 days, showing himself to them by many "infallible proofs."[29] Paul the apostle recounts that Yeshua appeared to more than 500 of his followers at one time, the majority of whom were still alive and who could confirm what Paul wrote.[30]

The empty tomb was "too notorious to be denied." Paul Althus states that the resurrection "could have not been maintained in Jerusalem for a single day, for a single hour, if the emptiness of the tomb had not been established as a fact for all concerned."[31]

The theories advanced to explain the resurrection from natural causes are quite weak; they actually help to build confidence in the truth of the resurrection.

The Wrong Tomb. A theory propounded by Kirsopp Lake assumes that the women who reported the body gone mistakenly went to the wrong tomb. If so, then the disciples who went to check up on the women's statement must have also gone to the wrong tomb. However, we may be certain that the Jewish authorities, who asked for a Roman guard to be stationed at the tomb to prevent the body being stolen, would not have been mistaken about the location, nor would the Roman guard, for they were there!

If this were the case, the Jewish authorities would have lost no time in producing the body from the proper tomb, thus effectively quenching for all time any rumor of a resurrection.

Another attempted explanation claims that the appearances of Yeshua after the resurrection were either illusions or hallucinations. Unsupported by the psychological principles governing the appearances of hallucinations, this theory also does not coincide with the historical situation. Again, where was the actual body, and why wasn't it produced?

Swoon Theory. Popularized by Venturini several centuries ago and often quoted today, the swoon theory says that Yeshua didn't really die; he merely fainted from exhaustion and loss of blood.

Everyone thought him dead, but later he was resuscitated and the disciples thought it to be a resurrection.

The skeptic David Freidrich Strauss—himself certainly no believer in the resurrection—gave the deathblow to any thought that Yeshua revived from a swoon:

> It is impossible that a being who had stolen half-dead out of the sepulcher, who crept about weak and ill, wanting medical treatment, who required bandaging, strengthening and indulgence, and who still at last yielded to his sufferings, could have given to the disciples the impression that he was a Conqueror over death and the grave, the Prince of Life, an impression which lay at the bottom of their future ministry. Such a resuscitation could only have weakened the impression which he had made upon them in life and in death, at the most could only have given it an elegiac voice, but could by no possibility have changed their sorrow into enthusiasm, have elevated their reverence into worship.[32]

The Passover Plot by Hugh Schoenfeld gives a modern rendition of the swoon theory.

The Body Stolen?   Then consider the theory that the body was stolen by the disciples while the guard slept.[33] The description and cowardice of the disciples provide a hardhitting argument against their suddenly becoming so brave and daring as to face a detachment of soldiers at the tomb and steal the body. They were in no mood to attempt anything like that.

J. N. D. Anderson has been dean of the faculty of law at the University of London, chairman of the department of Oriental law at the School of Oriental and African Studies and director of the Institute of Advanced Legal Studies at the University of London. Commenting on the proposition that the disciples stole Yeshua's body, he says:

> This would run totally contrary to all we know of them: their ethical teaching, the quality of their lives, their steadfastness in suffering and persecution. Nor would it begin to explain their dramatic transformation from dejected and dispirited escapists into witnesses whom no opposition could muzzle.[34]

The theory that the Jewish or Roman authorities moved Yeshua's body is no more reasonable an explanation for the empty tomb than theft by the disciples. If the authorities had the body in their possession or knew where it was, why, when the disciples were preaching the resurrection in Jerusalem, didn't they explain: "Wait! We moved the body—Yeshua didn't rise from the grave"?

And if such a rebuttal failed, why didn't they explain exactly where his body lay? If this failed, why didn't they recover the corpse, put it on a cart, and wheel it through the center of Jerusalem? Such an action would have destroyed the resurrection message—not in the cradle but in the womb!

Dr. John Warwick Montgomery further explains, "It passes credibility that the early [followers of Yeshua] could have manufactured such a tale and then preached it among those who might easily have refuted it simply by producing the body."[35]

Professor Thomas Arnold, for 14 years the headmaster of Rugby, author of a famous three-volume *History of Rome* and appointed to the chair of Modern History at Oxford, was well acquainted with the value of evidence in determining historical facts.

This great scholar said, "I have been used for many years to study the histories of other times, and to examine and weigh the evidence of those who have written about them, and I know of no one fact in the history of mankind which is proved by better and fuller evidence of every sort, to the understanding of a fair inquirer, than the great sign which God hath given us that [Yeshua] died and rose again from the dead."[36]

Brooke Foss Westcott (1825-1901), an English scholar, said, "Taking all the evidence together, it is not too much to say that there is no historic incident better or more variously supported than the resurrection. Nothing but the antecedent assumption that it must be false could have suggested the idea of deficiency in the proof of it."[37]

Dr. Paul L. Maier, professor of ancient history at Western Michigan University, concludes that: "If all the evidence is weighed carefully and fairly, it is indeed justifiable, according to the canons of historical research, to conclude that the tomb in which Jesus was buried was actually empty on the morning of the first Easter. And no shred of evidence has yet been discovered in literary sources, epigraphy or archaeology that would disprove this statement."[38]

Changed Lives.   But the most telling testimony of all must be the lives of those early disciples. We must ask ourselves: What caused them to go everywhere telling the message of the risen Messiah?

Had there been any visible benefits accruing to them from their efforts—such as prestige, wealth, increased social status or material benefits—we might logically attempt to account for their actions, for their wholehearted and total allegiance to this "risen Messiah."

As a reward for their efforts, however, these early disciples were beaten, stoned to death, thrown to the lions, tortured, crucified— every conceivable method was used to stop these men from talking.

Yet, they were the most peaceful of men, who physically forced their beliefs on no one, but rather indeed laid down their lives as the ultimate proof of their complete confidence in the truth of their message.

A believer in Yeshua today can have complete confidence, as did those first believers, that his faith is based, not on myth or legend, but on the solid historical fact of the risen Messiah and the empty tomb.

Most important of all, the individual believer can experience the power of the risen Messiah in his life today. First of all, he can know that his sins are forgiven.[39] Second, he can be assured of eternal life and his own resurrection from the grave.[40] Third, he can be released from a meaningless and empty life and be transformed into a new creature in Yeshua.[41]

What will be your evaluation and decision—what think you of the empty tomb?

APPENDIX B: RESPONDING TO QUESTIONS AND OBJECTIONS

Various questions or problems may trouble the Jewish person about Yeshua's message, and he might raise some objections. In responding to these, keep in mind several important principles.

1. Don't argue; show love and tact.

2. Agree with him when he has made a good point.

3. If you don't have an answer, admit it and promise to find out.

4. Refer constantly to the Jewish Bible.

5. After responding, bring the conversation back to Yeshua—his atonement, the relationship with God he provides, and the necessity to accept him as Messiah. In this way you can better relate your responses to those major issues.

6. Be careful not to pressure—or appear to pressure—your friend to accept Yeshua. Your role is to present an alternative which he must choose to accept, reject or consider further.

Doesn't Belief in Yeshua Mean You're No Longer Jewish?

A. *Not at all. Belief in Yeshua is Jewish and was meant to be Jew-*

ish. That is why we talk about Messianic Judaism.
B. *The founder and early leaders of the Messianic Jewish faith were Jewish. They lived and practiced as Jews.*
1. Yeshua was Jewish.
a. He was born and lived as a Jew, consistently following the traditions (Gal 4:4; Jn 8:46).
b. He taught others to observe the customs (Mt 23:3).
2. The disciples worshiped daily in the Temple (Acts 2:46; 3:1, etc.).
3. Paul was Jewish.
a. He observed the customs such as vows and purification (Acts 18:18; 21:24, 26).
b. He kept the feasts (Acts 20:5-6, 16; 27:9; 18:21 in some manuscripts).
c. He followed the traditions and practices of the law (Acts 25:8; 28:17).
d. He described himself and his practices as *strictly* Jewish (Acts 21:39; 23:1, 6; 26:5).
4. James was Jewish. Josephus records that the apostle James was greatly respected by the devout Jews because of his devotion to Judaism. When the high priest had him killed, the Pharisees protested so strongly to Rome that they removed the high priest.
5. The apostles were all Jewish. Irenaeus, a second-century church leader, wrote: "But they themselves continued in the ancient observances. Thus did the apostles scrupulously act according to the dispensation of the Mosaic law."
C. *The Messianic Jewish faith uses Jewish Scriptures.*
1. The Tenach (Old Testament) is the basis for teaching and belief (Jn 5:46-47).
2. The B'rith Hadasha (New Testament) was written by Jewish authors to explain Jewish teachings.
D. *Its teachings are Jewish.*
1. Yeshua taught that he came to fulfill, not set aside, the Jewish faith; he warned others against setting it aside (Mt 5:17-19).
2. Paul told Jewish followers of Yeshua to remain Jewish (1 Cor 7:18) and spoke of his message as that which the Jewish Scriptures taught (Acts 26:22).
3. Some of these Jewish teachings include:
a. Atonement based on the exchange-of-life principle (compare

Lev 17:11 and 2 Cor 5:21);
b. A personal relationship with God (Jn 1:12; compare Ezek 36: 25-27; Jer 31:31-33);
c. The promised Messiah of Israel;
d. The Tenach as the revelation of God;
e. The unique unity of God (Deut 6:4; compare Mk 12:23-30).
4. In fact, the first theological controversy (Acts 15) was whether a Gentile could be a true follower of Yeshua without being or becoming Jewish.
E. *Prediction and anticipation in the Tenach point toward the Messianic Jewish faith.*
1. Isaiah 52:13—53:12; Daniel 9:24-26. A coming Messiah.
2. Deuteronomy 18:18-19. A future prophet.
3. Jeremiah 31:30-33. A new covenant.
F. *The Romans regarded Yeshua's followers as a Jewish sect because they couldn't distinguish between them and other Jews.*
G. *Modern scholarship understands the Jewishness of Yeshua.*
1. David Flusser, department head at Hebrew University and author of the article on Yeshua in the *Jewish Encyclopedia:* "As a Jew he fully accepted the Law. The community he founded, comparable in some ways to the Essenes, saw itself as a movement of reform and fulfilment within Judaism, not as a secession from it."[1]
2. Martin Buber, philosopher and author, writes: "I am more than ever certain that a great place belongs to him in Israel's history of faith and that this place cannot be described by any usual categories."[2]

Why Don't the Rabbis and the Jewish People Accept Yeshua?

A. *Many Jewish people including rabbis and Jewish leaders have accepted Yeshua as Messiah.*
1. According to Neander, a Jewish historian, by the end of the first century CE there were one million Jewish believers in Yeshua in Israel alone.
2. Today there are many that believe also. A rabbi has estimated that two to three thousand Jewish people each year accept Yeshua. Some of them have formed the Messianic Jewish Alliance of America with its approximately twenty member branches. It is part of the International Hebrew Christian Alliance, which has about

fifteen member nations.

3. A prominent Orthodox rabbi, Isaac Lichtenstein of Hungary, publicly acknowledged his acceptance of Yeshua early in this century. Many of his congregation followed his example.

4. Dr. Max Wertheimer was a Reform rabbi and graduate of Hebrew Union College. He accepted Yeshua as Messiah and wrote of his experience in his tract, "How a Rabbi Found Peace."

5. Dr. Paul Levertoff had a congregation of about seven hundred Jewish followers of Yeshua in London.

6. Joseph Rabinowitz of Kishinev (Russia) had a following of several thousand Messianic Jews.

B. *Furthermore, today many Protestant and Catholic religious leaders don't accept Yeshua as Messiah and Savior. They reject him as the way of salvation. Why should Jewish leaders be any different?*

C. *You know, Moses was rejected by the people of Israel and her leaders (Ex 17:1-4; 32:9-10; Num 11:14-15).*

D. *The prophets of God were rejected by Israel and her leaders (Jer 25:4).*

E. *If Moses and the prophets were rejected, why should it be any different for the Messiah?*

1. In fact, it was predicted that he would be rejected by his people (Is 53:3-4).

2. He didn't come as they expected, as a great political conqueror and hero; he came as a humble servant to atone for sins (Zech 9:9; Is 53).

3. Israel and her leaders couldn't understand this. God promised that they wouldn't be able to understand because of their spiritual condition (Is 6:9-10; 29:10-11).

4. Throughout Jewish history it was a minority of Jews who obeyed God. The prophets called this minority the remnant (1 Kings 19:10, 18; compare Is 1:9). The majority, by and large, including the religious leaders of the day, turned from God's revelation.

F. *Another important consideration is the Jewish understanding of the unity of God. In many cases the composite unity of God—often called the Trinity—has been misrepresented and poorly communicated. In addition, rabbinic modifications of the biblical concept of monotheism have clouded the issue. For example,*

Maimonides referred to God as *yachid* (absolute oneness) instead of the biblical *echad* (composite unity).
G. *Actually, Jewish people have been brought up to disbelieve Yeshua. Rabbi Samuel Sandmel of Hebrew Union College admitted: "I must be straightforward in saying that my approach is partisan; it is Jewish and not neutral."* [3]
H. *Remember, rabbis are human; they're not infallible. The final authority for the identity of the Messiah should rest with the Jewish Scriptures.*

If Yeshua Was Really the Messiah, Why Didn't He Bring Peace to the World?

A. *The argument: "The Jewish Messiah was to be the great ruler who would initiate and institute a new world order of peace and justice. In his time all men will be sensitive to God, and there will be no evil. Yeshua did not do any of this."*
B. *The answer: "If the Jewish Messiah came and people refused to accept him, he couldn't very well bring peace, could he?"*
C. *Saadya Gaon, a great rabbi and leader of the tenth century, said concerning the coming of Messiah: "Israel was exiled because of sin; God will bring even greater suffering on Israel to pressure Israel to repentance so that she will be redeemed."*
D. *Moses laid down this same principle (Lev 26:40, 42): Israel must first acknowledge her iniquity and sin; then God will grant her the blessings of his covenant with Abraham and the benefits of Messiah's reign (Jer 3:13-18).*
E. *The consistent teaching of the Jewish Scriptures is that the Jewish people must recognize their sinful condition and repent before they can be restored to enjoyment of God's blessings.*
1. Messiah will not bring peace and justice into the world by some magic force, regardless of the spiritual condition of the Jewish people.
2. Even the Talmud says: "Rabbi Yehoshua ... asked Messiah: When will my Master come? Messiah answered him: Today. He then returned to Elijah. .... Yehoshua objected: He lied to me for he said he is coming today and behold he did not come. The prophet Elijah explained: He said it in this way: Today—if you hear his voice." [4]

3. Before there can be peace in the world, man must have peace with God—a proper, harmonious relationship with God—and peace within himself.

F. *Ezekiel 36:25-28 illustrates this. Prior to Messianic benefits and the restoration of the intimate relationship between God and his people (v. 28), two things must happen: cleansing and forgiveness from sin (v. 25); then, a new nature and new inclinations (vv. 26-27). In other words, redemption and Messianic blessings without repentance and regeneration (change of nature and character) is spiritually unthinkable and morally impossible. Man would then only spoil it. To suggest otherwise ignores the holiness and justice of God (see Jer 4:1-2).*

G. *Daniel 9:24-26. How is this forgiveness of sins with its consequent new nature to be brought about?*

1. This prophecy concerns the coming of the anointed one, the Messiah (vv. 25-26).

2. The purpose of his coming was "to make an end of sins, make reconciliation [or atonement] for iniquity, and bring in everlasting righteousness" (v. 24).

3. This means Messiah is to accomplish the conditions of Ezekiel 36:25-28, the prior conditions for Messianic blessing and a right relationship with God.

H. *Isaiah 53:5-6, 8, 11-12. How is Messiah going to accomplish these conditions; in other words, how will he forgive sins and bring about the consequent new nature?*

1. This passage (Is 52:13-15) speaks of God's servant, who will be exalted. These are descriptions of Messiah (Is 42:1; 49:6).

2. Messiah would bear the sins of Israel and the world; they would be placed on him by God (vv. 5-6, 11-12).

3. By his death (v. 8) he would atone for the sins of Israel and the world. The result would be forgiveness of sins and a proper relationship with God (vv. 11-12). (Also see pp. 125-33, "How to Present the Principles of Atonement.")

I. *Therefore, before Messiah could ever bring peace, he had to bring about the conditions which God required as prerequisites for Messianic blessings. These conditions required his death as an atonement for sins so that man could be cleansed of sin and given a new nature.*

1. The first time he came in a humble fashion (Zech 9:9) to die as an atonement for sins.

2. He will return to rule, at which time he will be recognized as "the pierced one," the one who did die as an atonement for sins (Zech 12:10; Is 53:10-12). The writings of the rabbis also reflect this twofold mission: "Like the first redeemer so will the final redeemer be. The first redeemer was Moses, who appeared to them and then disappeared.... For he will disappear from their sight and will then again appear to them."[5]

3. In the meantime he waits for men to respond to his provision for sin, giving them the opportunity to enter a proper relationship with God (Hos 5:15). The Day of Atonement prayer *Oz M'lifnai B'reshit* speaks of Messiah in the same way (see p. 179).

Where Does the Jewish Bible Ever Mention That Messiah Comes Twice?

A. *The Jewish Bible doesn't* explicitly *say Messiah comes twice.*

B. *However, our sages and rabbis have long puzzled over certain things said by our Scriptures about the Messiah. They apparently realized that several passages spoke of some suffering that Messiah would undergo (e.g., Is 50:4-10; 52:13-15; Zech 12:10; Ps 22: 14-18; Dan 9:24-27).*

C. *As they wrestled with this problem, they came to a solution.*

1. The ultra-Orthodox of the first century, the Essenes of the Dead Sea community, concluded that there were two Messiahs: one "from Aaron" and one "from Israel." One was apparently a priestly Messiah, having to do with sacrifice and atonement, while the other was a royal Messiah.[6]

2. The rabbis came to a similar conclusion. There was Messiah ben David (Son of David) and Messiah ben Yoseph (Son of Joseph). The first was to rule, the second to die. The Talmud bears this out: "It is clear that it refers to Messiah ben Yoseph who was killed." (Sukkah 52a). Some among today's Orthodox still hold to this view.

D. *However, Yeshua suggested a different alternative when he spoke of himself as the Messiah, one Messiah coming twice. But if this view is a correct understanding of Scripture, the Jewish Bible should give some indication of this.*

E. *Several passages describe a Messianic character, God's ser-*

vant, who may have been the model for the Messiah ben Yoseph.
1. Isaiah 42:1-4.
a. What is this person called (v. 1)? *God's servant.*
b. What has God put upon him? *His spirit.*
c. What does he do in the earth (v. 4)? *Judge it.*
2. Isaiah 49:5-6.
a. Whom has God formed from the womb (v. 5)? *His servant.*
b. What is the servant to do (vv. 5-6)? *Bring Israel back to God, raise up and restore Israel, make God's salvation known to the world.* This sounds a lot like the functions of the Messiah.
F. *Several passages describe the Messiah in ways parallel to these descriptions of the servant.*
1. Isaiah 11:1-9.
a. Who is described (v. 1)? *A rod out of Jesse, a branch.* These are terms which designate the Messiah. Compare Jeremiah 23:5-6.
b. What will one of his functions be (v. 4)? *To judge the earth.*
c. What will be the result of his rule (v. 9b)? *The earth will be full of the knowledge of God.*
2. Ezekiel 37:22-24.
a. As Israel becomes one nation again, who will rule her (v. 22)? *One king.* This describes Messiah (compare the description in v. 24 if necessary).
b. What will be the result of Messiah's rule (vv. 23-24)? (Messiah is often called by the name of his forefather, David.) *The people will no longer defile themselves; they will be cleansed; they will again know and obey God.*
G. *Notice that the passages describing the Messiah exactly parallel those describing the servant (review the specific descriptions if necessary).*
H. *In yet other passages the two figures, servant and Messiah, merge.*
1. Zechariah 9:9.
a. Who is described? *The coming king.* In other words, the Messiah.
b. How is he described and what is he riding (v. 9b)? *Lowly, riding an ass's colt.*
c. Kings usually ride on horses; servants ride donkeys. The Messiah is pictured here as "lowly" and comes riding as a servant.

2. Zechariah 3:8-9.

a. Whom will God bring forth (v. 8b)? *His servant, the sprout of David.* "Sprout of David" refers to Messiah, as we saw in Isaiah 11. (Compare also Jer 23:5-6.) Here he is called the servant.

b. As a result of the Messiah's coming, what will God remove in one day (v. 9b)? *The iniquity of Israel.* So Messiah has something to do with removing iniquity; keep this in the back of your mind.

3. The Zechariah passages, when compared to the previous passages, show that the servant and Messiah are the same person. Therefore, Messiah has two distinct functions, to be king and to be servant. Apparently the latter relates to removing iniquity and to suffering.

I. *Several crucial passages intimate that these two functions of Messiah involve, not two different Messiahs, but one Messiah who comes to earth twice.*

1. Zechariah 12:8-10.

a. These verses refer, as do much of chapters 12—14, to the events at Messiah's coming: God defending Israel, the house of David (Messiah's lineage) being exalted, the spirit of grace being poured out on Jerusalem.

b. After Messiah pours out the spirit of grace, what do the people do (v. 10)? *Look at him.*

c. What do they do next? *Mourn.*

d. It's strange that the people should mourn at such a joyful time. The key to the mourning is found in how they see the Messiah when they look at him.

e. Words in italics are the editor's indication that these words are not in the original Hebrew text. Remembering this, see how Messiah is described when they look at him. *One whom they pierced.*

f. That this passage describes Messiah is clearly indicated by the Talmud passage quoted earlier (Sukkah 52a). The Talmud repeats this verse after making the identification with Messiah ben Yoseph quoted earlier.

2. Isaiah 49:7.

a. We already saw in verses 5-6 that Messiah is being described as a servant.

b. How is the servant treated by people and nations (v. 7a)? *Despised, abhorred.*

c. How will he be treated in the future (v. 7b)? *Kings and princes will worship him.*

d. Therefore, the Messiah undergoes a period of humiliation and suffering (his servant function) before being honored (his king function). This description sounds just like another passage of Scripture.

3. Isaiah 52:13-15.

a. Who is described (v. 13)? *God's servant.*

b. What will happen to him? *He will be exalted.*

c. So Messiah is definitely in view here. Prior to his being honored, why were many astonished at him (v. 14)? *His visage and form were marred terribly.* He apparently went through severe physical suffering before being honored.

d. Even kings are amazed at these events because they did not expect this to happen (v. 15).

e. Chapter 53 continues the same subject. Verse 1 indicates that these events that amazed even kings are not readily believed by many people.

f. In fact, how is Messiah treated (v. 3)? *Despised and rejected.* This again refers to his humiliation and suffering as a servant.

g. What happened to him because of our transgressions and iniquities (v. 5)? *He was wounded and bruised.* The Hebrew for wounded *(chalal)* literally means "pierced through" (as Zech 12: 10 has also described him).

h. What has God caused to fall on him (v. 6b)? *All of our iniquities.*

i. Why was he cut off or killed (v. 8b)? *Because of our transgressions.*

j. By his death what did he take off (v. 12b)? *The sins of many.* (See Zech 3:9 on Messiah's relationship to removing iniquity.)

k. In other words, Messiah's suffering as a servant involved his dying as an atonement for our sins. (Compare sections E and F of "How to Present the Principles of Atonement" in Appendix A, pp. 125 to 133, for fuller discussion, if necessary, and for the complete discussion as to whom the passage is referring to.)

l. In verse 9, the terms *grave* and *tomb* show that Messiah not only dies but is buried.

m. After he is dead and buried, what happens to Messiah's "days" (v. 10b)? *God prolongs them.*

n. How can his days (or life) be prolonged when he is already dead and buried? *He must come back to life.*
o. What happens next? *God's program prospers in his hand.* This refers to his exaltation which we already saw in 52:13 and 49:7.
4. In other words, Messiah suffers and dies in humiliation as a servant and atones for sin. He then rises from the dead. At some future time he will return and rule as part of God's program, at which time he will be recognized as the "pierced one" (Zech 12:10).
5. The writings of the rabbis also reflect this twofold mission: "Like the first redeemer so will the final redeemer be. The first redeemer was Moses, who appeared to them and then disappeared. . . . For he will disappear from their sight and will then again appear to them."[7]
J. *What happens in the meantime? Hosea 5:15 might give a hint.*
1. What will he do? *Go and return to his place.*
2. For how long? *Until they acknowledge their offense and seek his face.*
3. An ancient Yom Kippur musaf prayer from the Jewish prayer book, *Oz M'lifnai B'reshit,* echoes the same thought as it virtually quotes Isaiah 53.

> The Messiah our righteousness has turned from us. We are alarmed, we have no one to justify us. Our sins and the yoke of our transgressions he bore. He was bruised for our iniquities. He carried on his shoulders our sins. With his stripes we are healed. Almighty God, hasten the day that he might come to us anew; that we may hear from Mt. Lebanon a second time through the Messiah, who is called Yenon.

K. *He awaits each of us to acknowledge our sins and his sacrifice as this explains. (Go to point 5 in L'chaim.)*

Why Do Christians Worship Three Gods?

A. The argument: *"You talk about Father, Son and Holy Spirit, three Gods. We worship only one God."*
B. *The answer: "We do believe in one God. In fact, we got our belief in one God from you."*
C. *The only certain way we can know about God is from what he said about himself in the Bible.*
D. *Even with this knowledge, the nature of God is a mystery; it is*

inscrutable (Is 55:8-9).

E. The Shema: *Deuteronomy 6:4.*

1. Many Jewish interpreters do not take the *Shema* as an ontological statement (one which describes God's being) at all. They translate it, "The LORD is our God, the LORD alone," meaning that Israel has only one God.

2. Even if the *Shema* is describing God's being, we should recognize that the Hebrew word for one used here is *echad,* a word which strongly implies composite character. The other Hebrew word for one is *yachid,* used to imply absolute oneness. The famous Hebrew scholar and rabbi Maimonides recognized this distinction. He accordingly changed the word to describe God to *yachid* instead of *echad.*

3. *Echad* in the Jewish Bible.

a. Genesis 2:24. "They shall become one flesh." The union of two persons is referred to as one.

b. Numbers 13:23. "Branch with a single cluster of grapes." *Single* here refers to composite unity. Not one grape (absolute unity), but many grapes in one cluster.

c. Ezekiel 37:17. "They [the two sticks for Israel and Judah] shall become one in thy hand." Two become one, a composite unity.

4. *Yachid* in the Jewish Bible.

a. Genesis 22:2. "Take your only son." In God's eyes Abraham had only one son, Isaac, the son who had been promised.

b. Jeremiah 6:26. "Mourning as for the only son." Only one is in view (compare Zech 12:10).

c. Judges 11:34. "She was his only child." He had no other.

5. Since *echad* is used in Deuteronomy 6:4, it is reasonable to say that God's essence or nature is composite. The Zohar, the great book of Jewish mysticism, makes an interesting comment on this passage: "Why is there need of mentioning the name of God three times in the verse? The first Jehovah is the father above. The second is the stem of Jesse, the Messiah who is to come from the family of Jesse through David. And the third one is the way which is below, and these three are one."

F. *There are other hints of this mysterious composite unity.*

1. Genesis 1:26-28. "Let us make man in our image, after our likeness." God is a complexity in unity such that man was created male-female to adequately reflect the image of God. God didn't picture himself by creating a solitary man (compare Eccles 12:1; Ps 149:2; Is 54:5; where the descriptive terms used of God are plural).

2. Isaiah 48:12-17.

a. The speaker is the one who called Israel, who is the first and the last (v. 12). In verse 13 he is described as the creator.

b. Who does this refer to? *God.*

c. The speaker is then described as the one who has been in existence from the beginning. Who does this refer to (v. 16, read till "there am I")? *God.*

d. God the creator is still speaking in the last part of verse 16. What does he say? *The Lord God and his Spirit have sent me.* Two persons are described as doing the sending! Two divine persons are said to have sent God the creator!

3. Psalm 45:8.

a. Italics indicate words supplied by the translator but which are not in the Hebrew text.

b. Whose throne is forever (v. 7)? *God's.*

c. The same person, God is being addressed in verse 8. Yet, there is reference to his (God's) God. Compare Psalm 110:1, 4, where "master" translates the Hebrew word *Adonai,* "Lord," and this Lord is described as an *eternal* priest.

4. Zechariah 2:14-15 (verses 10-11 in some versions).

a. Who will dwell in the midst of Zion (v. 14)? *The Lord.*

b. As the Lord dwells in the midst of his people, what will they know (v. 15)? *The Lord of hosts has sent him (the Lord).* The Lord of Israel is sent by the Lord of hosts!

5. Malachi 3:1.

a. In the last line of verse 1, who is speaking? *The Lord of hosts.*

b. Whom will he send (first line)? *My messenger.*

c. As this messenger comes to the Temple, how is he described? *The Lord, the messenger of the covenant.* So the Lord of hosts' messenger is the Lord.

d. Several ancient Jewish scholars also saw this interesting correlation.

(1) Rabbi Ibn Ezra: "The Lord is both divine majesty and the angel of the covenant, for the sentence is doubled."

(2) Rabbi David Kimchi: "The Lord is King Messiah. He is also the

angel of the covenant."[8]

How Can Yeshua Be God?

A. The argument: "The Tenach leaves no room for a God-man. God never takes on a human form."

B. The Bible indicates several times that God took on a human form.

1. Exodus 24:9:11.

a. Moses and Aaron, Nadab and Abihu and seventy elders went up.

b. Whom did they see in verses 10 and 11? God!

2. Genesis 18.

a. Whom did Abraham see (v. 2)? Three men.

b. What was the identity of one of them (v. 1)? The Lord! (Compare verses 13-14.)

c. Two of the men leave and Abraham stands before the Lord (the third man) and speaks to him (vv. 22-33)!

3. Genesis 32:25-30.

a. Who is Jacob wrestling with (v. 25)? A man.

b. Jacob asked the wrestler what his name was, and he was blessed by the wrestler (v. 30).

c. Whom did Jacob say he saw and wrestled with (v. 31)? God, face to face.

4. Isaiah 6:1. Whom did Isaiah see in all his majesty? The Lord.

C. The Tenach gives many other instances which comport with the idea of God in human form.

1. Proverbs 30:4 (read to "what is his name?").

a. Who is this talking about? God.

b. (Read the rest, "What is his son's name?") Then God has a son!

c. Compare Psalm 2 which speaks of the "anointed one," the literal translation of Messiah (v. 2), and describes him as the king of the earth (vv. 6, 8). In verse 7, what is Messiah called? God's son.

2. Joshua 5:13-15.

a. Who was the man Joshua encountered (v. 14)? The captain of the host of the Lord.

b. What was Joshua's response to this discovery? He bowed down and worshiped him! Would Joshua have worshiped anyone but God? No. Exodus 20:5 forbids the worship of anyone other than God. Notice that the captain did not refuse the worship.

c. What did Joshua call the captain? *Lord.*

d. What was Joshua told to do (v. 15)? *Take off his shoes because he was on holy ground.* In Exodus 3:5-6 this is exactly what Moses was told. He was told to do so because he was in the presence of God.

3. Judges 13:8-23.

a. To whom did Manoah speak (v. 11)? *The man who had talked to his wife.*

b. After the encounter with this man, Manoah and his wife discovered they were talking to whom (v. 22)? *God!* (Note their fear; compare Ex 33:20 and Judg 6:21-25.)

4. Exodus 23:20-22.

a. Whom would God send to guide Israel (v. 20)? *An angel.*

b. What was Israel told to do (v. 21)? *Obey him and not provoke him.*

c. Why? *Because if they did not obey him, he wouldn't pardon their transgressions.*

d. Can anyone but God forgive sins? *No.* (Refer to Is 43:25; Ps 130: 4; Dan 9:9 if necessary.)

5. The king of the earth.

a. Zechariah 14:9. Who will be king over all the earth? *The Lord.*

b. Daniel 7:13-14.

(1) Who is described as coming out of the clouds (v. 13)? *The son of man.*

(2) What was given to him (v. 14)? *A kingdom.*

(3) What is the extent of his kingdom? *All nations.*

(4) How long would he rule? *Forever.*

(5) Therefore, the son of man (Messiah) is king over the earth!

c. Compare Psalm 2.

(1) Who is the object of the rebellion (v. 2)? *The Lord and his anointed* (anointed = Messiah).

(2) What is the extent of Messiah's rule as king (vv. 6, 8-9)? *The uttermost parts of the earth.*

(3) Therefore, Messiah is king over the earth.

d. Since according to Zechariah 14:9 the Lord is king over the earth, then Messiah must be the Lord!

D. *Micah 5:1; Isaiah 7:14; 9:5-6. Messiah as deity. (See the discussion on these passages, Appendix A, pp. 133-140.)*

If There Is a God, Why Did He Allow Six Million Jews to Die?
A. The argument: "If there is a loving God, he never would have allowed that kind of suffering and outrage."
B. The answer: "That is a difficult question; there is no simple answer. It's hard to explain and hard to understand."
C. God has not been caught by surprise by the suffering of the Jewish people through the ages. During the time of Moses, he specifically predicted the suffering and persecution the Jewish people would face in foreign countries if they chose to disobey God and, as a consequence, went into exile (Lev 26; Deut 28, 32).
D. Rather than think of the six million killed, think of the twelve million left alive. The Holocaust can be viewed as a massive and diabolical attempt to thwart the purposes of God with regard to the Jewish people (see Rev 12:10-17). If Hitler or the Czars had had their way, there would be no Jews left alive today. But God has preserved the Jewish people through almost four thousand years of history, as he promised (see Deut 4:31).
E. We dare not view this question as if the Holocaust was all we knew about the Jewish people and God. Despite this horror, "the exodus did not turn into a mirage; Sinai has not come tumbling down; the prophets have not become charlatans; the return from Babylon has not proved to be a fairy tale."[9] God has acted throughout Jewish history, and even in our generation has brought the Jewish people back to Israel just as he promised.
F. "But what was God doing during the Holocaust?" God was mourning. He was mourning over the dead, the persecuted and those whose minds were scrambled with the lust for power.
G. God was suffering along with each act of violence.
H. "But then why did he sit back and let it happen?"
I. God made man with the ability to make decisions.
1. He gave man the power to choose love, to choose peace, to choose humility.
2. Instead, man has chosen hatred, war and pride.
3. God mourns over poor choices but does not violate our ability to decide; God treats us as adults, respecting our decisions.
J. In the world that we as mankind have collectively built, it was a set of historical and moral decisions that permitted the Third Reich to grow. Most of these were decisions to "play dumb," to

not care, to look on the misery of other human beings as somebody else's business, and not our own. We repeatedly see the same unwillingness to get involved today.

K. The Holocaust, then, is not a dilemma about God, but about man. "The Holocaust proved not that God was dead, but that man's humanity to man was dead. Man is given the freedom to choose: ... [the Nazis] chose to exercise unbridled evil; ... the world chose to exercise indifference."[10]

L. We have responded to the privilege of decision-making with a timeline full of irresponsible choices.

M. God will eventually judge man for his decisions (Dan 12:2; Ps 37:7-11; 73:10-20). What will be the result of God's judgment of your life? (Review L'chaim.)

I Don't Want Any Part of the New Testament. It's Anti-Semitic.

A. That's a pretty common assumption. But you wouldn't expect Jewish people to be anti-Semitic. The New Testament, or B'rit Hadasha, was written by Jews.

B. In fact, as one biblical scholar observed,

There is no foundation for the accusation that a seed of contempt and hatred for the Jews can be found in the New Testament. . . . Some of the books of the New Testament may bear the marks of the conflict between the young church and the synagogue, but no degradation of the Jewish people, no unjust accusation, no malevolent prophecy is ever suggested or implied.[11]

C. The crucifixion of Yeshua is often blamed on the Jewish people as a justification for anti-Semitism.

1. While the B'rit Hadasha acknowledges the responsibility of elements of the Jewish leadership in Yeshua's death, it does not single them out as chiefly responsible.

2. Acts 4:27. Who was responsible for Yeshua's death? Herod, Pilate, Gentiles and people of Israel.

D. Some people cite Yeshua's denunciation of the Pharisees in Matthew 23 as an example of anti-Semitism.

1. But his criticism is very Jewish, as Dr. David Flusser of Hebrew University points out:

All the motifs of Jesus' famous invective against the Pharisees in Matthew xxiii are also found in rabbinical literature. Both in

Jesus' diatribe and in the self-criticism of the rabbis the central
polemical motif is the description of the Pharisees as being
prone to hypocrisy. Jesus says that "they make up heavy loads
and lay them on men's shoulders... " (Matt. xxiii:4). In the
Talmud we read about five types of Pharasaic hypocrisy; the
first is to "lay the commandments upon men's shoulders" (Jer.
Berakhoth 14b).[12]
2. Jeremiah 23:9-15. The great prophets of Israel spoke against
their own people in much the same way.
a. How are the people in the land described (v. 10a)? *Adulterers.*
b. How are the prophets and priests described (v. 11a)? *Profane.*
c. How are the prophets described here (v. 14)? *They commit adul-
tery, walk in lies, strengthen evildoers, are like Sodom and Go-
morrah.*
E. *The Gospel of John is often criticized as anti-Semitic because of
its derogatory use of* the Jews.
1. Upon close inspection, we see that John uses this term in a number of ways and with a variety of meanings. It can refer either to
Yeshua's audience (Jn 8:31; 11:45; 12:11) or to the religious authorities (1:19; 6:52).
2. In the passages describing the controversy between Yeshua
and the religious leaders, the term usually refers to the antagonistic
Pharisees (1:19, 24) or to the chief priestly establishment or Sanhedrin (18:12; 19:12-15). Since these specific people are viewed as
opposing God and his Messiah, they are naturally cast in an un-
favorable light. This is no more anti-Semitic than the statements
of the prophets mentioned earlier.
3. The historical and cultural background of John and the Gospel
add further insight into the use of the Jews.
a. John and almost all the disciples were from Galilee. The inhabitants of Jerusalem and Judea, and especially the religious
hierarchy, often ridiculed the Galileans for their religious and
social crudeness. For Galileans, applying the term the Jews in a
somewhat sarcastic way to their more self-assured and smugly
religious counterparts would be customary.[13]
b. The Gospel of John has many similarities in language and
thought to the writings of the Dead Sea community, Qumran.
Many of these writings include protests against the Temple priest-

hood and the religious establishment, who are viewed as corrupt and in rebellion against God. Drawn from a somewhat similar background and perspective, the Gospel shares a similar criticism of the religious leadership.[14]

4. Several passages from the Gospel illustrate this specific use of *the Jews.*

a. John 7:10-13 describes Yeshua's appearance in Jerusalem at the Jewish holiday, Sukkot (the Feast of Tabernacles).

(1) What group of people is mentioned (v. 11)? *The Jews.*

(2) What group is described here (v. 12)? *The multitudes (crowds).*

(3) The crowds are viewed in distinction to *the Jews.* And yet, at this Jewish feast in Jerusalem the crowds are certainly as Jewish as *the Jews,* which here refers to the religious leadership (v. 13).

b. John 9:13-22 describes the aftermath of Yeshua's healing of a blind Jewish man in Jerusalem.

(1) What group is mentioned as part of *the Jews* (vv. 16-18)? *The Pharisees.*

(2) Who is afraid of *the Jews* (v. 22)? *The blind man's parents.* But the parents were Jews.

(3) Why were they afraid? *The Jews might throw them out of the synagogue.*

(4) Only the religious leadership had this power. The term *the Jews* is to be equated with the religious hierarchy and not the Jewish people as a whole.

F. *The apostle Paul is occasionally criticized for his derogatory references to* the Jews.

1. Yet a close examination of his use of the term reveals the same usage as the Gospel of John, as a reference to the religious establishment.

2. Acts 28:17-20 describes Paul's actions in Rome after his arrival. He was in Rome because of accusations made by the religious leaders in Jerusalem (v. 17).

a. Whom did he call together (v. 17)? *The leading men of the Jews in Rome.*

b. Whose objection forced his appeal to Caesar (v. 19)? *The Jews'.*

c. *The Jews* here again indicates the religious establishment in Jerusalem as opposed to those to whom he is speaking. A look at the passage describing the situation Paul referred to quickly validates this identification of the Jews as the religious hierarchy (Acts 25:1-11; compare also 23:14-20).

G. *An examination of the B'rit Hadasha clearly shows that the charges of anti-Semitism are false. In fact, if anything, it elevates and honors the Jewish people and their place in God's program (see Jn 4:22; Rom 3:1-2; 9:1-5; 11:26-27).*

I Don't Need a Mediator (Go-Between); I Can Approach God Directly.

A. *The argument: "Judaism teaches that no intermediary is necessary to approach God. We don't need a priest or saint to speak to God for us; we do it for ourselves."*

B. *The answer: "A priest or saint isn't necessary to speak to God for us. Man can approach God directly. But he must do so on God's terms. The Jewish Bible indicates how this can be done."*

C. *We have to admit that Moses played the part of a mediator between Israel and God on a number of occasions.*

1. Exodus 32:10-14, 30-32.

a. What was God's reaction to Israel's gross idolatry (v. 10)? *He was going to consume (destroy) them.*

b. What did Moses do (vv. 11-12)? *He begged (besought) God not to destroy Israel.*

c. What was the result (v. 14)? *God didn't destroy Israel.*

d. What did Moses hope to do to counteract the people's "great sin" (v. 30b)? *Go to God and make atonement for the sin.*

e. What did he ask God to do if God wasn't ready to forgive the people's sin (v. 32b)? *Blot him (Moses) instead of the people out of God's book.* The book referred to is probably the Book of Life (Ps 69:29; Mal 3:16-17).

f. Psalm 106:23 is the commentary on this incident. Why didn't God destroy Israel? *Moses stood in the breach and turned away God's wrath.*

2. Deuteronomy 9:23-26; 10:10.

a. What had Israel done (9:23)? *Rebelled against God.*

b. Why did Moses fall down before God and pray (9:25-26a)? *So that God wouldn't destroy Israel.*

c. What was the result of Moses' intervention or mediation (10:10)? *God did not destroy Israel.*

D. There were others who also played the part of mediators between God and Israel.
1. Numbers 25:9-13. God brought a plague on the people of Israel because of gross sin. Phinehas intervened.
a. What was the result of Phinehas's action in this situation (v. 11)? *He turned away God's wrath and Israel wasn't destroyed* (compare Ps 106:29-30).
b. How did God describe the result of Phinehas's zealousness for God (v. 13b)? *He made atonement for Israel.*
2. Numbers 17:9-13 (16:44-48 in some translations).
a. Once again Israel is in gross rebellion against God and God is about to judge them (vv. 9-11).
b. What did Aaron do after he ran into the center of the congregation (v. 12)? *Put on incense and made atonement for the people.*
c. What was the result of his action (v. 13)? *The plague stopped.*
E. There were ways in which the priesthood fulfilled the function of mediation for Israel (Num 18:1, 5; compare 3:10). As part of their function, the prophets were also to intervene between man and God (Deut 18:15-16; compare Ex 20:18-19).
F. Therefore, the idea of mediation or intervention between man and God is certainly not foreign to the Jewish Bible. The early extrabiblical Jewish writings make use of this idea as well. The Targums are Aramaic translations and explanations of the Jewish Bible which date back almost to the time of Ezra. They attribute to Abraham, Moses and others the office of mediator with God. The Targum on the Song of Songs (Canticles) provides several good examples:
1. Canticles 1:5 describes Moses going up into heaven and taking with him peace between Israel and her God and King.
2. Canticles 2:15 explains that it was the sacrifice which Abraham offered in Isaac that ultimately induced God not to destroy Israel for its sin with the golden calf.
3. Targum Jonathan commenting on Zechariah 12:5 describes the Messiah as Redeemer of Israel in much the same way as a mediator with God.[15]
G. The giving of the great covenant that God made with the Jewish people at Mt. Sinai is also instructive.
1. Exodus 20:18-19. God gives the Ten Commandments or Words

with the people standing around Mt. Sinai.

a. What did the people see and hear (v. 18)? *Thunder, lightning, trumpets, the mountain smoking.*

b. What was their response (v. 19)? *They asked Moses rather than God to speak to them.*

c. Why didn't they want God to speak to them? *They were afraid they'd die.*

2. Deuteronomy 5 gives more details about this incident. The people of Israel heard a voice and saw the mountain on fire (v. 20).

a. What did they realize (v. 21a)? *God had shown his glory and greatness and had spoken to them.*

b. What was their fear (v. 22b)? *If they heard the voice of God again, they would die.*

c. What did they request (v. 24)? *That Moses hear what God had to say and then tell them what God said.*

d. God agrees to the request, sends the people away and tells Moses what to say to them (vv. 27-28).

e. How did Moses describe his position in this situation (v. 5a)? *I stood between the Lord and you.* This is the precise definition of mediation.

H. *Through the prophets God revealed that he would establish another covenant with Israel.*

1. Jeremiah 31 describes this covenant.

a. What is this covenant called (v. 30)? *A new covenant.*

b. What will God do as part of this new covenant (v. 32b)? *Put his law in our inward parts, write it on our hearts, be our God.*

c. What else will he do (v. 33c)? *Forgive our sins.*

d. What will be the end result (v. 33b)? *Everyone will know God.* In other words, under the new covenant there will be direct, unhindered access to God.

2. Daniel 9 tells us how the new covenant is established.

a. What is the purpose of the seventy weeks (v. 24)? *To finish transgression, make an end of sin, make reconciliation for iniquity, bring in everlasting righteousness;* in other words, to produce the results associated with the new covenant.

b. Whose coming is mentioned in connection with producing these results (v. 25)? *The anointed, the prince.* The Hebrew word for anointed is the word for Messiah, so Messiah's coming is described.

c. What happens to the Messiah, the anointed (v. 26a)? *He's cut off or killed.*

d. So Messiah's coming and death are related to the establishment of the new covenant.

3. Isaiah 53 expands the relationship between Messiah's death and the results of the new covenant (see the discussion on Isaiah 53, pp. 130-33, if needed). There his death is described in terms of atonement and mediation (for example, in verses 5-6, 12).

4. It shouldn't be surprising that mediation and atonement are part of the new covenant since both are part of the covenant made at Mt. Sinai (for further discussion, see pp. 127-33 on atonement).

I. *Remember, Moses acted as mediator in the giving of the covenant at Mt. Sinai. Similarly, Messiah is described as the mediator of the new covenant (see Heb 9:15; 12:24). Messiah's death as an atonement for sin opened up the new covenant blessings to us so that we can now have direct, unhindered access to God.*

J. *The way for us to secure this access to God and participate in new covenant blessings is relatively simple. (Go to L'chaim, the "Relationship with God" approach on pp. 154-62, or "Principles of Atonement" approach on pp. 125-33.)*

Why Do I Have to Ask Messiah into My Life? I Already Pray and Admit My Sins to God. I Have My Own Religion.

A. *Warning: Don't say anything which might sound like you are challenging or questioning the fact that your friend is sincerely following God to the best of his ability.*

B. *I certainly respect your religion and try to understand it. (Mention things that you admire about his religion, such as ethics, endurance through persecution and family closeness.)*

C. *However, we are not talking about another religion. We want to share a personal relationship with God which we learned about from the Jewish Bible. Our faith is in a person described by the Hebrew Scriptures.*

D. *There is nothing wrong with the spiritual exercises of repentance, prayer and good deeds; they demonstrate a concern for one's self and for society. But we must keep them in their proper perspective.*

E. We must look to the Jewish Bible as the final "court of appeals" on how to have a proper, personal relationship with God. (Go into L'chaim or one of the approaches found in Appendix A.)

How Can You Be So Sure Yeshua Is the Messiah?
A. That's a good question and a very legitimate one.
B. The Jewish Bible must be our final authority on this issue. Moses and the prophets predicted many things about the Messiah. The one who fits their descriptions and fulfills their prophecies is Messiah.
C. Let's see what the Jewish Bible says about Messiah. (Go through the "Messianic Prophecy" approach found in Appendix A, pp. 133-140.)

How Can Yeshua Rightfully Claim David's Throne?
A. The argument: "If Yeshua was really born of a virgin and Joseph wasn't his real father, he has no right to be the Messiah and king. That right comes through the father."
B. To make a proper decision on that we must find out if a woman can receive and transmit inheritance rights according to the Jewish Bible.
1. Numbers 27:3-8. Zelophehad died and had no sons. His daughters came to Moses and asked that they be given the inheritance of their father. Moses agreed with their reasons and gave them the inheritance. In 27:8 he was commanded by God to tell Israel: "If a man dies without a son, his inheritance passes to his daughter." Thus women had property and inheritance rights.
2. Judges 4—5. Women had administrative rights as well. Deborah the prophetess exercised leadership and delivered Israel from the Canaanites. Under her administration God gave Israel peace from their enemies for forty years.
3. 2 Kings 11. Queen Athaliah ruled Judah for six years. She was overthrown, not because she was a woman, but because she seized the throne through murder and intrigue.
4. Queen Salome-Alexandra ruled Israel from 76-67 BCE and proved to be a wise and beneficial ruler. She healed some of the political divisions and kept Israel free from invasion during this time.

5. Numbers 36:6-7. Daughters without brothers could receive family inheritances provided they did not forfeit these rights by marrying into another tribe. Many biblical scholars believe that Mary was a descendant of David through Nathan; Joseph through Solomon. So she married into the same tribe and retained her inheritance rights. Since there is no record of her having a brother, the inheritance of Heli (Mary's father) was hers. In fact, even the Talmud expressly speaks of her as the daughter of Heli (Chagiga 77d).

C. *2 Samuel 7:12-16. God's promise to David.*

1. God promised David that his throne would be forever.

2. Yet Jeremiah 22:30 says of Jeconiah, one of Solomon's descendants, that none of his descendants would ever rule Judah.

3. The promise of an eternal throne was given unconditionally to David, not Solomon (see 1 Chron 28:6-7 and 1 Kings 11:9-13). Therefore, David's kingly inheritance and rights might later be transmitted through some other line than that of Solomon and Jeconiah.

4. 1 Chronicles 3:5. Although Solomon was older than Nathan (2 Sam 12:24), this list places Nathan before Solomon, perhaps indicating that Nathan was in some way greater than Solomon. Mary, the mother of Yeshua, was a descendant of Nathan (Lk 3)!

Why Do Christians Hate and Persecute the Jews?

A. *Every true Christian should feel grieved over the persecution which has been inflicted on Jewish people in the name of Yeshua.*

1. This is a gross violation of the commands of Yeshua and the B'rit Hadasha.

2. It has resulted in a misrepresentation of the message of the B'rit Hadasha and a lack of awareness of the Messiahship of Yeshua.

B. *It's essential to realize that not every Gentile is a Christian, even if he attends church regularly.*

1. According to the teachings of Yeshua and the B'rit Hadasha, a person has to make a faith commitment to Yeshua in order to be a genuine Christian (Jn 3:16-18; Eph 2:8-9).

2. Therefore, a man isn't born a Christian, nor does he become one by attending a church; becoming a Christian involves a moral decision on his part to personally accept Yeshua as Savior and Messiah.

3. It's possible for a person to know the facts of the B'rit Hadasha and the ministry of Yeshua, and yet never have committed himself to Yeshua.

a. This commitment is called a spiritual birth (Jn 3).

b. It results in a changed nature (2 Cor 5:17).

c. Many people who are called Christians and attend churches have never experienced this spiritual birth.

C. *Most of those who have persecuted the Jewish people in the past have been these so-called Christians who have not experienced spiritual birth and a changed nature, so they are incapable of loving others as Yeshua commanded.*

D. *Yeshua commanded his followers to love all men (Mt 5:44). The message of the B'rit Hadasha is integrally related to loving others (1 Cor 13). In fact, Gentile Christians are specifically told to be thankful to the Jewish people for their own relationship with God (Rom 9–11).*

E. *A consistent, genuine Christian will obey the commands of Yeshua and the B'rit Hadasha. He will love his fellow man (Jn 13:35) and will demonstrate his love by doing good to others (Gal 6:10).*

Why Do You Try to Convert Us? Preach to Your Own People! They Need It.

A. *The message we're communicating is not that Jews should convert and become Gentiles. Like the ancient prophets, we say to the Jewish people, "Return to the God of your fathers. Return and experience the relationship with God that's available through the Messiah." This doesn't rob a person of his Jewishness; it heightens it. (If necessary, refer to the first question, pp. 169-71.)*

B. *You are right, though, that the Gentiles need to hear the message of Yeshua, and we need to share the message with them also.*

C. *Optional: Use this section with care and love. The Christian church learned its philosophy of evangelism from the Jewish system of the first century.*

1. The Jewish people were actively proselytizing until the fifth century. They had a whole system of proselytizing which included a specific procedure for turning a Gentile into a Jew.[16] Several texts indicate this:

a. Matthew 23:15.
b. Tacitus *History* 5. 5.
c. Josephus *Antiquities* 18. 3. 5 and 20. 2. 4; also *Jewish Wars* 2. 17. 10ff. and 2. 20. 2.
d. Midrash: Bereshith Rabba 39; Vayyikra Rabba 1. According to these texts, every proselyte was to be regarded as if a soul had been created.
2. God had intended for the Jewish people to proselytize when he called them a light and a witness (Is 42:6; 43:10-12; 44:8; 49:6).
3. Messianic Jews picked this up and communicated Yeshua's message first to their own people and then to the Gentiles.
4. So when Gentile Christians evangelize, they are doing what they learned originally from the Jews.
D. *However, the purpose of biblical faith is to give all people the opportunity to share in the atonement available through the Messiah. That means the biblical faith is a universal message.*
1. To offer this message to all people and not to the Jews would be a highly discriminatory act.
2. The Jew has a right to hear this message. May I share it with you? (Go through *L'chaim.)*

We Don't Believe in Original Sin. How Can Man, Thousands of Years after Adam, Be Held Responsible for Adam's Sin?

A. *Original sin means that because of Adam's transgression, the effect of his disobedience is passed on to his descendants.*
1. This means that man today has a nature which is sinful, and he sins because he has this sinful nature.
2. The Jewish objection: this puts man in an unfair position.
a. He suffers because someone else disobeyed.
b. This view binds a person to his nature.
B. *Jewish thought teaches that it is entirely possible for man to live an exemplary life and make decent moral choices.*
C. *Agree: It is possible for man to lead a good moral life, to practice beautiful ethics, to raise the level of society, and to help his fellow man.*
D. *However, man must face God.*
E. *What do the Jewish Scriptures say about our relationship with God?*

1. Man's heart or nature is deceitful, wicked, sinful (Jer 17:9; Ps 51:7). Even the Jewish writings acknowledge this when they speak of the *yetzer ha-ra* ("evil inclination") in man.
2. All men have sinned (Eccles 7:20; Ps 14:2-3; 53:3-4).
3. All men have turned their backs on God and gone their own way (Is 53:6).
4. God cannot tolerate and overlook sin; he must deal with it if he is to be a just God. He judges and rejects it (Hab 1:13; Nah 1:3; Ps 5: 5-7; Num 14:18; Jer 31:29; Ezek 18:4).
5. Thus, there is a barrier between God and man (Is 59:1-2).
6. Man cannot obtain God's righteousness and a proper relationship with God through his own efforts (Is 64:5; Ps 143:2; Ps 49:8-9, 16; Ezek 33:12-13).
F. *Even the Ten Commandments demonstrate this; they act like a mirror. When a man breaks one or more of the commandments, he can see he is a transgressor.*
G. *So God provided the sacrificial system and the sin offering. This system showed that man could not satisfy God's demands for righteousness through his own efforts; the sacrifice had to be brought and the animal had to die. On the basis of the exchange-of-life principle, sin was dealt with and atonement was made. (Go through the Principles of Atonement approach, pp. 125-33, or L'chaim.)*

We Believe in Treating People with Love; We Want to Live at Peace with One Another Now. We Don't Worry about the Hereafter.

A. *We agree wholeheartedly with the first two statements. This is why we share mutual concerns with our Jewish friends—to indicate our love and concern. We are vitally interested in them as a people, in their land, and in the problems they face. Together with them we too are striving for a world of peace.*
B. *But how are love and peace to be achieved? The Jewish Scriptures explain why people don't love the way they ought to and why we don't have peace.*
1. The Jewish Bible speaks of a sinful nature and the sins people commit as a result of rebellion. (Ps 51:7; Eccles 7:20; Is 53:6; Jer 17:9; also see the previous question if necessary.)
2. When a person receives God's righteousness, his entire nature

is changed, and he can behave properly toward his fellow man (Ps 51:11-12; Jer 31:32-33; Ezek 36:25-27).

3. God's righteousness enables man to demonstrate the greatest genuine care and concern. He is given (by virtue of a new nature) a new dynamic, the power of God which enables him to carry out his highest resolves (Ezek 36:25-27).

C. *There is, however, something more. This encounter with the righteousness of God, which comes through the Messiah, has eternal consequences; it produces a relationship with God that lasts forever.*

1. Only the person who has the righteousness of God can enjoy God's presence forever.

2. If a man dies without appropriating the righteousness of God, he will be severed from God's presence (Jer 31:29; Hab 1:13; Ezek 18:4).

3. We need an encounter with God's righteousness to safeguard our eternal destiny and to receive the power by which we can live the most useful lives here and now. This is accomplished through what we call the exchange-of-life principle. (Go through *L'chaim* or the Principles of Atonement approach, pp. 125-33.)

Does the Jewish Bible Teach Life after Death?

A. *Don't preach hell to him; it will turn him off. The apostles didn't and were highly successful (see the gospel messages in Acts).*

B. *The "real you" isn't just your body; there is something beyond the physical. It's the spirit or "the breath of life" (Gen 2:7).*

C. *You continue to live after your present body has ceased to exist.*

1. Job 19:26-27; 14:7, 14. Job said he would see God after he died.

2. Isaiah 26:19; 66:24; 24:22 (cf. Eccles 3:17; 12:14) all speak of life after death.

3. Daniel 12:2. Everyone will experience a resurrection resulting in either everlasting life or everlasting shame and contempt.

I Don't Need the New Testament.

A. *If appropriate, use the notes on "I Have My Own Religion," pp. 191-92.*

B. *Answer: "I understand your sentiments. Being familiar with the Jewish Scriptures, you of course realize that much of it points* forward to things in the future."

1. The prophets continually predicted God's actions in the future, such as national deliverance, a Messiah and individual cleansing.

2. Moses promised a greater prophet to come (Deut 18:15-19).

3. Jeremiah predicted that God would enact a new covenant, or testament (31:30-33).

4. Therefore, the Jewish Scriptures indicate that there will be a future revelation and communication from God.

C. *Really, I wanted to talk to you from the Jewish Scriptures. They have some very important things to say about our lives. (Go through L'chaim or the "Relationship with God" approach, pp. 154-62.)*

Notes

Chapter 1: Why Communicate the Biblical Message?
[1]Scholars are not in agreement here, but William F. Albright says that *"every book of the New Testament was written by a baptized Jew"* (*Christianity Today*, January 1963, p. 18, emphasis mine).
[2]For further explanation of the exchange-of-life principle, see Louis Goldberg, *Our Jewish Friends* (Evanston, Ill.: Moody Press, 1977), pp. 90ff.
[3]Richard DeRidder, *My Heart's Desire for Israel* (Philadelphia: Presbyterian and Reformed Press), pp. 93, 97.
[4]Oswald T. Allis, *Prophecy and the Church* (Philadelphia: Presbyterian and Reformed Press, 1945).
[5]Franz Delitzsch, *Allgemeine Evangelisch-Lutherische Kirchenzeitung* (1896), col. 552ff.
[6]Rabbi Stanley Rubinowitz, quoted by Susan Perlman in "The Furor over Jewish Evangelism," *Eternity*, April 1973, p. 22.

Chapter 2: The Jewish People in the Program of God
[1]I am grateful to Dr. Ralph Alexander and to Mal Couch for stimulating my thinking in this area.

Chapter 3: Aspects of the Jewish World View
[1]Some of the material in this chapter was gleaned from the following: Benjamin Efron, ed., *Currents and Trends in Contemporary Jewish Thought* (New York: KTAV, 1965); Louis Jacobs, *Jewish Theology* (New York: Behrman House, 1973); Alfred Jospe, *Tradition and Contemporary Experience* (New York: Schocken Books, 1970); Beldon Menkus, *Meet the American Jew* (Nashville: Broadman Press, 1963); Stuart Rosenberg, *Judaism* (New York: Paulist Press, 1966); Solomon Schechter, *Aspects of Rabbinic Theology* (New York: Schocken Books, 1972).
[2]Milton Steinberg, *Basic Judaism* (New York: Harcourt, Brace & World, 1947), p. 73.
[3]Quoted in Solomon Schechter, *Aspects of Rabbinic Theology*, p. 313.
[4]Compare Milton Himmelfarb, *The Jews of Modernity* (New York: Basic Books, 1973).

Chapter 4: A Survey of Church-Synagogue Relations
[1]Chrysostom *Homily* 1. 4-6; 4; 5.
[2]Letter to the Duchess of Brabant, *De Regimine Principum;* see also *Summa Theologica.*
[3]Martin Luther, *Concerning the Jews and Their Lies.*
[4]John Calvin, *Corpus Reformatorum,* see 40:605; 50:307; 41:167; 25:665; 35:616.
[5]One such example, Gary Allen and Larry Abraham, *None Dare Call It Conspiracy* (Seal Beach, Calif.: Concord Press, 1972), merely repeats the Protocols views in a modern setting.
[6]Hilaire Belloc, *The Jews* (London, 1928), pp. 73, 210.
[7]Lucy Dawidowicz, *The War against the Jews* (New York: Bantam Books, 1976), pp. 219-20.
[8]Johann Snoek, *The Grey Book* (New York: Humanities Press, 1970), p. vi.
[9]Franz Delitzsch, *Allgemeine Evangelisch-Lutherische Kirchenzeitung (1896).*
[10]*Near East Report,* 1 January 1982.
[11]*Broward Jewish Journal,* 7 October 1982; *Chicago Sun-Times,* 24 May 1981.
[12]*Chicago Daily News,* 10 November 1979.
[13]*St. Petersburg Times,* 10 October 1982; *Newsweek,* 23 August 1982, pp. 32-35.
[14]*Chicago Sun-Times,* 6 January 1982.
[15]*St. Petersburg Times,* several issues in September-October 1982.
[16]Leonard Fein, "Notes on the New Anti-Semitism," *Moment,* December 1981, pp. 61-63.
[17]*Time,* 25 November 1974, pp. 16-19.
[18]*Christian Victory,* December 1975, p. 58. Surveys taken through the summer of 1982 show that this figure has remained steady or has perhaps somewhat increased.
[19]*New York Times,* 3 November 1975.
[20]Gertrude J. Selznik and Stephen Steinberg, *The Tenacity of Prejudice* (New York: Harper & Row, 1971), p. 108.
[21]Arnold Foster and Benjamin Epstein, *The New Anti-Semitism* (New York: McGraw Hill, 1974), p. 324.
[22]Jules Isaac, *Jesus and Israel* (New York: Holt, Rinehart & Winston, 1959), p. vi.

[23]Augustin Cardinal Bea, *The Church and the Jewish People* (New York: Harper & Row, 1966), p. 87.

[24]Notes from the course, "The Life and Ministry of Jesus," taught by R. T. France at Trinity Evangelical Divinity School, Deerfield, Ill., Spring 1975.

[25]*Time*, 25 November 1974, p. 19.

[26]Quoted in Selznik and Steinberg, *The Tenacity of Prejudice*, pp. 12-13.

[27]Andrew Greeley, "Ethnicity, Denomination and Equality," *Church and State*, December 1975, p. 15.

[28]Stephen Isaacs, *Jews and American Politics*, quoted in *Time*, 25 November 1974, p. 19.

Chapter 5: The Jewish People and the Land

[1]Quoted in Louis Goldberg, "Is God a Zionist? A Case for Zionism," *Amood Esh*, April 1976, p. 1.

[2]A. Koestler, *Promise and Fulfillment*, p. 17.

[3]Letter to Felix Frankfurter, 5 March 1919, quoted in Walter Laqueur, *The Israel-Arab Reader* (New York: Bantam Books, 1970), pp. 21-22.

[4]*Middle East Information Series* (Israel Information Centre), p. 8.

[5]*The Hebrew Christian*, Winter 1974, p. 152.

[6]*Jewish Press*, 28 February 1974, p. 3.

[7]*Near East Report*, 28 January 1976, p. 14.

[8]*Middle East Background* (Consulate General of Israel, 1975).

[9]*Near East Report*, 29 January, 26 February, 12 March 1982.

[10]*Israel, Jordan, and the Palestinians* (Consulate General of Israel, 1974).

[11]See Larry Collins and Dominique Lapierre, *O Jerusalem* (New York: Simon and Schuster, 1972), and dispatches from Aubrey Lippincott, U.S. Consul in Israel.

[12]*Israel, Jordan, and the Palestinians.*

[13]*Jerusalem Post*, 1 August 1969.

[14]*Christianity Today*, 6 October 1978, p. 23.

[15]*Israel, Jordan, and the Palestinians.*

[16]*Trouw*, 3 March 1977.

[17]*American Hebrew Christian*, Spring 1975, p. 26.

[18]Quoted in *Near East Report*, 7 January 1976, p. 3.

[19]Ibid.

[20]*Commentary*, February 1976, quoted in *Near East Report*, 18 February 1976.

[21]*London Daily News*, February 1976, quoted in *Near East Report*, 18 February 1976.

[22]Quoted in *Near East Report*, 30 June 1976, p. 113.

[23]*Near East Report*, 7 July 1976, p. 115.

[24]*Washington Post*, 16 November 1974.

[25]*Stern*, July 1981.

[26]*Al-Jazira*, 8 January 1982.

[27]*Near East Report*, 5 February 1982.

[28]Max Nurock, *Information Briefing* (Israel Information Centre, July 1975), pp. 1-2; "Sixty Minutes," 24 September 1978.

[29]Msgr. John Osterreicher, "Zionism and National Aspirations," speech made in Chicago, Ill., 28 April 1976; see also *Near East Report*, 17 September 1982, p. 185.

[30]*Near East Report*, 24 March 1976, p. 49.

[31]*Altneuland*, quoted in *Near East Report*, 18 February 1976.

[32]Letter to Felix Frankfurter, quoted in Walter Laqueur *The Israel-Arab Reader* (New York: Bantam Books, 1970), pp. 21-22.

[33]*Near East Report*, 21 January 1976, p. 10.

[34]Extracted from *Near East Report*, 26 February 1982, p. 43.

[35]*Near East Report*, 25 June 1980, p. 126. The material in this section and the next three was compiled from the following sources: Leonard Fein, "Days of Awe," *Moment*, September 1982; Peter Hellman, "Diary of an Unholy War," *Rolling Stone*, 14 October 1982; Danny Siegel, "Pomegranates and Other Words for Our Time," *Moment*, September 1982; CBS "Eleven O'Clock News," 21 September 1982; *Broward Jewish Journal*, 7 October 1982; *Chicago Sun-Times*, 26 June 1982; *Jerusalem Post*, 11-17 July 1982; *Near East Report*, 25 June 1980; 11 June; 2, 9, 16, 23, 30 July; 6, 13, 20 August; 3, 17 September; 1, 8 October 1982; *Neighborhood Newspaper* (Tampa), 9 September 1982; *St. Petersburg Times*, 3, 4, 21 September; 9 October 1982; *Samaritan's Purse World Medical Mission Newsletter*, August 1982; *Sh'ma*, 3, 17 September; 1 October 1982.

[36]*Samaritan's Purse World Medical Mission Newsletter*, August 1982, p. 3.

[37]*Near East Report*, 8 October 1982, p. 200.

[38]See King Fahd's interview quoted earlier in the chapter. Compare *Near East Report*, 30 July 1982, p. 155.

[39]Hubert Humphrey, speech, 3 May 1976, quoted in *Near East Report*, 2 June 1976.

[40]Some of the material in this paragraph was gleaned from the *Near East Report*, 9 October 1981, 22 January, 2 April, 15 October 1982.

[41]*Near East Report*, 15 October 1982, p. 207.

[42]*Near East Report*, 2 April 1982, p. 63.

[43]Speech at Maruf Saad camp in Sidon, Lebanon, 3 January 1982, broadcast by the Voice of Palestine, quoted in *Near East Report*, 22 January 1982, p. 19.

Chapter 6: The Influence of Two Wars

[1]Many of the insights in this chapter come from Patrice Fischer, "The Quest for Jewish Survival in America since 1967 and the Evangelical Community" (M.A. thesis, Trinity Evangelical Divinity School, June 1976).

[2]Emil Fackenheim, *Quest for Past and Future* (Bloomington, Ind.: Indiana University Press, 1968), p. 24.

[3]Norman Podhoretz, "A Certain Anxiety," *Commentary*, August 1971, p. 6.

[4]Emil Fackenheim, "Jewish Faith and the Holocaust," *Commentary*, August 1968.

[5]*Moment*, November 1979.

[6]Velvel Greene, speech before Jewish college students in Chicago, March 1973.

[7]Richard Rubinstein, *My Brother Paul* (New York: Harper & Row, 1972), p. 116.

[8]See, for example, George Otis, *The Ghost of Hagar* (Van Nuys, Calif.: Time-Light Books, 1974).

[9]Henry Knight, "The Yom Kippur War," *The Hebrew Christian*, Summer 1974,

p. 64.

[10]Greene, speech.

[11]Rabbi Stanley Rubinowitz, quoted by Susan Perlman in "The Furor over Jewish Evangelism," Eternity, April 1973, p. 22.

[12]Eugene Borowitz, How Can a Jew Speak of Faith Today? (Philadelphia: Westminster, 1969), p. 208.

[13]Eliezer Berkovits, Faith after the Holocaust (New York: KTAV, 1973), p. 24.

[14]M. G. Bowler, "The Hebrew Christian and the Church," American Hebrew Christian, Spring 1975, pp. 16-17.

[15]Antiquities 20. 9. 1.

[16]Against Heresies 3. 23. 15.

[17]Harry Siegman, quoted by James Hefley in "Everyone's Talking about These Jewish Christians," Moody Monthly, May 1973, p. 27.

[18]Samuel Fishman, Jewish Students and the Jesus Movement (Washington, D.C.: B'nai B'rith Hillel Foundation, 1973), p. 47.

[19]Rabbi David Polish, column in Jewish Sentinel, 7 October 1976, p. 13.

[20]"Jewish Identity," National Jewish Population Study (New York: Council of Jewish Federations and Welfare Funds, December 1974).

[21]John Fischer, "If It Be of God . . . " (Chicago: Messianic Jewish Alliance of America, 1977).

[22]R. Alan Cole, The Epistle of Paul to the Galatians (Grand Rapids, Mich.: Eerdmans, 1964), p. 12.

[23]Phil Goble, Everything You Need to Grow a Messianic Synagogue (South Pasadena, Calif.: William Carey Library, 1974), p. 10.

[24]W. Bauer, A Greek-English Lexicon of the New Testament and Early Christian Literature, trans. and ed. W. F. Arndt and F. W. Gingrich (Chicago: University of Chicago Press, 1957), s.v. plēroō.

[25]B. F. Westcott, The Epistle to the Hebrews (Grand Rapids, Mich.: Eerdmans, 1970), pp. lviii, lxi.

[26]Messianist is the exact equivalent of Christian, only using the Hebrew term rather than the Greek as its base.

Chapter 7: Principles of Communicating the Biblical Message

[1]Milton Steinberg, Basic Judaism (New York: Harcourt, Brace & World, 1947), pp. 31-33.

[2]"Jewish Identity," National Jewish Population Study (New York: Council of Jewish Federations and Welfare Funds, December 1974), pp. 2-4.

[3]Quoted in American Messianic Jewish Quarterly, Winter 1976, p. 6.

[4]Gunther Plaut, Your Neighbor Is a Jew (Philadelphia: United Church Press, 1968), p. 83.

[5]Quoted in James Hutchens, "A Case for Messianic Judaism" (D. Miss. dissertation, Fuller Theological Seminary, 1974), p. 74.

[6]Marshall Sklare, "Conversion of the Jews," Commentary, September 1973, pp. 44-53.

[7]See chapter 6, pp. 81-82.

[8]André Schwarz-Bart, *The Last of the Just,* trans. Stephen Becker (New York: Atheneum, 1973), pp. 364-65.

[9]See chapter 6, p. 82. Quotation is from Velvel Greene's speech before Jewish college students in Chicago, March 1973.

Appendix A: Using the Jewish Bible

[1]CE stands for common era. It is more acceptable to Jews than AD *(anno Domini),* which means "in the year of the Lord."

[2]Louis Goldberg, *Our Jewish Friends* (Evanston, Ill.: Moody Press, 1977).

[3]Makkoth 31d.

[4]Harry Orlinsky, ed., *The Fifty-third Chapter of Isaiah according to the Jewish Interpreters* 2:17.

[5]Daniel Juster, *A Messianic Congregation* (privately published pamphlet available from Congregation Or Chadash, P.O. Box 758, Palm Harbor, FL 33563).

[6]Goldberg, *Our Jewish Friends.*

[7]For a more complete discussion of major Messianic prophecies and for references to traditional Jewish writings citing these passages as Messianic, see *Footprints of the Messiah,* available from An Adventure in Faith, P.O. Box 758, Palm Harbor, FL 33563.

[8]Sanhedrin 98b.

[9]Sukkah 52a.

[10]Goldberg, *Our Jewish Friends.*

[11]"Toward a Troubled 21st Century," *Time,* 4 August 1980, p. 54.

[12]"Welcome to the 1980's," *SCP Newsletter* (Spiritual Counterfeits Project), February-March 1980, pp. 1-2.

[13]Wilhelm Gesenius, *Hebrew and English Lexicon;* compare C. F Keil and F. Delitzsch, *Biblical Commentary on the Old Testament* (Grand Rapids, Mich.: Eerdmans, 1973) 9:160.

[14]Berakoth 2:2; *The Mishnah,* trans. Herbert Danby (Oxford: Oxford University Press, 1938).

[15]Juster, *A Messianic Congregation.*

[16]For details on Jewish interpretation of Isaiah 53, see *Footprints of the Messiah* (An Adventure in Faith) or Orlinsky, *The Fifty-third Chapter of Isaiah According to the Jewish Interpreters.*

[17]2 Peter 1:16; 1 John 1:1-3; Acts 2:22; 26:24-26.

[18]F. F. Bruce, *The New Testament Documents: Are They Reliable?* (Downers Grove, Ill.: InterVarsity Press, 1964), pp. 44-46.

[19]William Albright, *Recent Discoveries in Biblical Lands* (New York: Funk and Wagnalls, 1955), p. 136.

[20]Josh McDowell, *Evidence That Demands a Verdict* (Arrowhead Springs, Calif.: Campus Crusade for Christ International, 1973), p. 46.

[21]Frederick G. Kenyon, *The Bible and Archaeology* (New York: Harper & Row, 1940), p. 288.

[22]Luke 1:1-3.

[23]Sir W. M. Ramsay, *The Bearing of Recent Discoveries on the Trustworthiness of*

the *New Testament* (London: Hodder & Stoughton, 1915), p. 222.

[24]John 19:39-40.

[25]Matthew 27:60.

[26]Mark 16:4.

[27]George Cume, *The Military Discipline of the Romans from the Founding of the City to the Close of the Republic* (an abstract of a thesis published under the auspices of the Graduate Council of Indiana University, 1928), pp. 41-43.

[28]A. T. Robertson, *Word Pictures in the New Testament* (New York: R. R. Smith, 1931), p. 239.

[29]Acts 1:3.

[30]1 Corinthians 15:3-8.

[31]Paul Althus, *Die Wahrheit des kirchlichen Osterglaubens*, pp. 22, 25ff.

[32]David Frederick Strauss, *The Life of Jesus for the People*, 2d ed. (London: Williams and Norgate, 1879) 1:412.

[33]Matthew 28:1-15.

[34]J. N. D. Anderson, *Christianity: The Witness of History* (London: Tyndale Press, 1969), p. 92.

[35]John Warwick Montgomery, *History and Christianity* (Downers Grove, Ill.: Inter-Varsity Press, 1964), p. 35.

[36]*Sermons on the Christian Life: Its Hopes, Its Fears, and Its Close*, 6th ed. (London: n. p., 1859), p. 324.

[37]Paul E. Little, *Know Why You Believe* (Downers Grove, Ill.: InterVarsity Press, 1968), p. 30.

[38]*Long Beach Independent Press-Telegram*, 21 April 1973, p. A-10.

[39]1 Corinthians 15:3.

[40]1 Corinthians 15:19-26.

[41]John 10:10; 2 Corinthians 5:17.

Appendix B: Responding to Questions and Objections

[1]David Flusser, *Jesus* (New York: Herder & Herder, 1969), p. 216.

[2]Martin Buber, *Two Types of Faith* (London: Routledge and Kegan Paul, 1951), pp. 12-13.

[3]Rabbi Samuel Sandmel, *We Jews and Jesus* (New York: Oxford University Press, 1973), p. 4.

[4]Sanhedrin 98.

[5]Numbers Rabba, on 11. 2.

[6]See *Cairo-Damascus Covenant* 12. 22—13.1; 14. 19; 20. 1; *Scroll of Discipline* 9. 11.

[7]Numbers Rabba, on 11. 2.

[8]Hal Lindsey, *The Promise* (Eugene, Ore.: Harvest House, 1982).

[9]Eliezer Berkovits, *Faith after the Holocaust* (New York: KTAV, 1973), p. 134.

[10]Shraga Arian, quoted in *The Second Jewish Catalog*, ed. Sharon and Michael Strassfeld (Philadelphia: Jewish Publication Society, 1976), p. 221.

[11]Gregory Baum, quoted in Edward Flannery, *The Anguish of the Jews* (New York: Macmillan, 1965), pp. 30-31.

[12]Flusser, *Jesus*, p. 225.

[13]For a detailed discussion of the tensions between the Jews of Galilee and those of Judea, see Geza Vermes, *Jesus the Jew* (London: Collins, 1973).

[14]For a study of the similarities between John and the Dead Sea writings, see Leon Morris, *Studies in the Fourth Gospel* (Grand Rapids, Mich.: Eerdmans, 1969).

[15]George Knight, *Jews and Christians* (Philadelphia: Westminster, 1965), pp. 126-27.

[16]For more information, see Bernard Bamberger, *Proselytism in the Talmudic Period*, rev. ed. (New York: KTAV, 1968).

Bibliography

History of the Jewish People
Grayzel, Solomon. *A History of the Jews.* New York: Mentor Books, 1968.
Sachar, Howard. *The Course of Modern Jewish History.* New York: Dell, 1958.

Jewish Thought and Religion
Bloch, Abraham, *Biblical and Historical Background of the Jewish Holy Days.* New York: KTAV, 1978.
Cohen, Abraham. *Everyman's Talmud.* New York: Dutton, 1949.
Donin, Hayim Halevy. *To Be a Jew.* New York: Basic Books, 1972.
Epstein, Isidore. *Judaism.* Baltimore: Penguin Books, 1959.
Gaster, Theodore. *Festivals of the Jewish Year.* New York: Sloane, 1953.
Greenstone, Julius. *The Messiah Idea in Jewish History.* Westport, Conn.: Greenwood Press, 1972.
Heilman, Samuel. *Synagogue Life.* Chicago: University of Chicago Press, 1976.
Heschel, Abraham. *God in Search of Man: A Philosophy of Judaism.* New York: Harper, 1955.
Kadushin, Max. *The Rabbinic Mind.* New York: Bloch, 1972.
——————. *Worship and Ethics.* New York: Bloch, 1963.
Klausner, Joseph. *The Messianic Idea in Israel.* New York: Macmillan, 1955.

Mielziner, Moses. *Introduction to Talmud*. New York: Bloch, 1969.

Montefiore, C. G., and Loewe, H. *A Rabbinic Anthology*. New York: Schocken Books, 1974.

Neusner, Jacob. *Invitation to the Talmud*. New York: Harper & Row, 1976.

——————. *The Way of Torah: An Introduction to Judaism*. Encino, Calif.: Dickenson, 1974.

Rosenberg, Stuart. *Judaism*. New York: Paulist Press, 1966.

Schechter, Solomon. *Aspects of Rabbinic Theology*. New York: Schocken Books, 1972.

Siegel, Richard; Strassfeld, Michael; and Strassfeld, Sharon. *The Jewish Catalogue*. Philadelphia: Jewish Publication Society, 1973.

Steinberg, Milton. *Basic Judaism*. New York: Harvest Books, 1947.

Strack, Hermann. *Introduction to the Talmud and Midrash*. New York: Atheneum, 1969.

Strassfeld, Michael, and Strassfeld, Sharon. *The Second Jewish Catalogue*. Philadelphia: Jewish Publication Society, 1976.

The State of Israel: History and Prophecy

Collins, Larry, and Lapierre, Dominique. *O Jerusalem*. New York: Simon and Schuster Pocket Books, 1972.

Kac, Arthur. *The Death and Resurrection of Israel*. Baltimore: King Brothers, 1969.

——————. *Rebirth of the State of Israel*. Evanston, Ill.: Moody Press, 1958.

Laqueur, Walter, ed. *The Israel-Arab Reader*. New York: Bantam Books, 1969.

The Modern Jewish Situation

Borowitz, Eugene. *The Mask Jews Wear*. New York: Simon and Schuster, 1973.

Cohen, Arthur, ed. *Arguments and Doctrines: A Reader of Jewish Thinking in the Aftermaths of the Holocaust*. New York: Harper & Row, 1970.

Foster, Arnold, and Epstein, Benjamin. *The New Anti-Semitism*. New York: McGraw-Hill, 1974.

Glazer, Nathan. *American Judaism*. Chicago: University of Chicago Press, 1972.

Himmelfarb, Milton. *The Jews of Modernity*. New York: Basic Books, 1973.

Jospe, Alfred. *Tradition and Contemporary Experience: Essays on Jewish Life and Thought*. New York: Schocken Books, 1970.

Sidorsky, David. *The Future of the Jewish Community in America*. New York: Basic Books, 1973.

Strober, Gerald. *American Jews: Community in Crisis*. Garden City, N.Y.: Doubleday, 1974.

Jewish-Christian Relations

DeLange, Nicholas. *Origen and the Jews: Studies in Jewish-Christian Relations in Third Century Palestine*. Cambridge: Cambridge University Press, 1977.

Eckhart, Roy. *Your People, My People: The Meeting of Jews and Christians*. New York: Times Books, 1974.

Fischer, Patrice. "A Quest for Jewish Survival in America Since 1967 and the Evangelical Community." M.A. thesis, Trinity Evangelical Divinity School, 1976.

Flannery, Edward. *The Anguish of the Jews.* New York: Macmillan, 1965.

Jocz, Jacob. *The Jewish People and Jesus Christ: A Study in the Controversy between Church and Synagogue.* London: SPCK, 1949.

Weiss-Rosmarin, Trude. *Judaism and Christianity.* New York: Jonathan David, 1943.

The New Testament and Jewish Backgrounds

Daube, David. *The New Testament and Rabbinic Judaism.* London: University of London Press, 1956.

Davies, W. D. *Paul and Rabbinic Judaism.* London: SPCK, 1970.

Goldberg, Louis. "The Deviation of Jewish Thought from an Old Testament Theology in the Inter-Testamental Period." Th.D. thesis, Grace Seminary, 1963.

Moore, George F. *Judaism in the First Centuries of the Christian Era.* Vol. 1. New York: Schocken Books, 1971.

Shurer, Emil. *History of the Jewish People in the Age of Jesus Christ.* 2 vols. Rev. and ed. Geza Vermes, Fergus Millar and Matthew Black. Edinburgh: T & T Clark, 1973.

Sigal, Philip. *The Emergence of Contemporary Judaism.* Pittsburgh: Pickwick Press, 1980.

Vermes, Geza. *Jesus the Jew.* London: Collins, 1973.

Jewish Believers and Messianic Judaism

Hutchens, James. "A Case for Messianic Judaism." D. Miss. dissertation, Fuller Theological Seminary, 1974.

Kac, Arthur. *The Messianic Hope.* Grand Rapids: Baker Book House, 1975.